THE
CROSS STITCH
BOOK

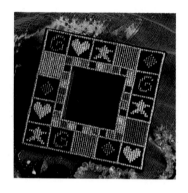

PRACTICAL HANDBOOK

THE
CROSS STITCH
BOOK

DOROTHY WOOD
Photographs by Lucy Mason

LORENZ BOOKS

Additional pictures in the book were reproduced with kind permission of the following libraries: Bridgeman Art Library, London p8; Embroiderers'' Guild p11, 12 (top left); Visual Arts Library, London p9 (top left); Witney Antiques, 96-100 Corn Street, Witney, Oxfordshire OX8 7BU p9 (right), 10, 12 (right), 13 (all except bottom right).

This edition published by Lorenz Books
an imprint of Anness Publishing Limited
Hermes House, 88-89 Blackfriars Road,
London SE1 8HA

Published in the USA by Lorenz Books
Anness Publishing Inc., 27 West 20th Street,
New York, NY 10011; (800) 354-9657

www.lorenzbooks.com

A CIP catalogue record for this book is available from the British Library

Publisher: Joanna Lorenz
Project Editor: Joanne Rippin
Designer: Janet James
Photographer: Lucy Mason
Charts: Ethan Danielson
Production Controller: Don Campaniello

Previously published as *The Ultimate Cross Stitch Companion*

Printed and bound in China

1 3 5 7 9 10 8 6 4 2

CONTENTS

INTRODUCTION 6

CHAPTER ONE
CELTIC AND MEDIEVAL 36

CHAPTER TWO
TRADITIONAL 90

CHAPTER THREE
FOLK ART 144

CHAPTER FOUR
CONTEMPORARY 200

INTRODUCTION

Embroidery, like many other traditional
pastimes, is currently enjoying a revival.
Cross stitch is a particularly easy and satisfying
skill to learn, relying only on neatness and
accuracy to produce simple as well as more
complicated designs.

The majority of cross stitch projects are
worked on evenweave fabric which allows
accurate counting and spacing of stitches. The
easiest fabric to use is Aida, where threads are
woven in blocks to facilitate sewing the cross
stitches. Aida is a very popular fabric both for
beginners and more experienced stitchers,
however in recent years linen-type fabrics have
also made a comeback. Although these fabrics
look more difficult to use, stitchers quickly get
used to counting the threads and the
professional finish is well worth the extra effort.

Many of the projects in this book use the
traditional stranded cotton but other threads
such as coton perlé and flower thread can also
be used to great effect. Whatever your level of
expertise, each project has been designed to
provide clear instructions and the useful
techniques section gives guidance on all aspects
of cross stitch.

Clear step-by-step photographs illustrate the
more complicated projects. You are also
encouraged to try other craft skills such as
sewing, painting and basic woodwork to
complete the designs and display the finished
cross stitch to its best advantage.

THE HISTORY OF CROSS STITCH

The Romans described embroidery as "painting with the needle". It was the Babylonians, however, who gave the technique its name. One of the oldest crafts, embroidery has been around for over 2,000 years.

During the late part of the nineteenth century and the early part of the twentieth century a great number of expeditions unearthed ancient tombs and burial grounds in Egypt and along the old trade routes. The excavations revealed many fragments of embroidered fabrics, although most disintegrated when they came into contact with the air.

There is very little embroidery in existence from before the twelfth century, although murals, sculpture, jewellery and later, illuminated manuscripts, inventories and paintings provide evidence of cross stitch and other embroidery having been produced.

Cross stitch evolved from the entirely practical double lacing of skins with thongs or gut, and developed over the years into a colourful and highly decorative craft. Almost every culture has employed cross stitch of one kind or another to decorate and embellish clothing and household items. Cross stitch and other forms of embroidery were used extensively in ceremonial decorations and regalia, and as such reflect the thoughts, ideas and religion of the people. Each country or area developed its own distinctive style of colour and pattern and had specific uses for cross-stitched fabric.

IN THE EAST

The nomadic tribes of India and Pakistan make exquisite multi-coloured bags and ornate hangings to hold and transport their belongings. These items are beautifully and ingeniously made with many hidden pockets. In Western Pakistan and Thailand cross stitch is used to decorate the yokes of garments and is traditionally stitched on black fabric using deep red and pink threads.

Chinese embroidery has always been highly prized, but there is insufficient evidence to show whether cross stitch embroidery actually originated in China or whether it was introduced from Persia, Greece and Egypt via the old trade routes. The "Silk Road" did undoubtedly contribute to the spread of cross stitch throughout the European continent.

Many geographically disparate countries share similar traditional designs such as the "key" or "fret" patterns. As a result it is difficult to determine the exact origin of many traditional motifs, but it is fascinating to see the different interpretations of various themes in the indigenous folk-art embroidery of countries as far apart as Spain and China.

LEFT: A picture of two women sewing together in an early fourteenth-century French manuscript.

ABOVE: In the eighteenth century women spent a lot of their time making and repairing the family linen. RIGHT: A band sampler with border patterns and alphabets. The positioning of the two animals indicates that the sampler was worked on the knee. (Whitney Antiques)

IN WESTERN EUROPE

Since the Middle Ages embroidery has been an important part of the decoration in churches and the homes of the nobility. From the twelfth until the fourteenth century English ecclesiastical embroidery was renowned throughout Europe. Much early embroidery was done by guilds of craftworkers or in convents and monasteries, but it was not until the beginning of the sixteenth century that counted thread embroidery became popular.

CANVAS WORK

With rising prosperity, there was a great demand for embellished clothes and furnishings as outward symbols of newly acquired wealth. Much was still done professionally, but as it now had a practical purpose, people from all walks of life tried their hands at embroidery, and many large European country houses had rooms filled with embroidered furnishings.

Chair seats, bed quilts, curtains, wall-hangings and even carpets were designed to imitate tapestries. These were stitched on canvas or linen in half cross stitch. Needlework pictures also became popular and embroidered book covers protected by linen bags stitched in canvas work were fashionable.

SAMPLERS

Early samplers were essentially a portable record of patterns and stitches worked on long strips of linen by amateur and professional stitchers. The samplers were kept rolled up in a sewing box and contained the types of stitches and patterns characteristic of the current costume and textiles. Later band samplers began to include alphabets and numbers and may have been used as a teaching aid for young children.

The shape of the sampler gradually became more square and the inclusion of a border pattern suggests that they were intended for display. During the eighteenth and nineteenth centuries young girls would have stitched at least one sampler during the course of their education. Samplers worked in charity schools and orphanages were typically stitched completely in red thread and were produced to help the girls to acquire the skills which would enable them to become a lady's maid. Samplers from this period generally contained text and pictures which were of a religious or moral nature. Biblical passages and psalms or hymns were popular, as were representations of Adam and Eve or the Tree of Life.

Over the years the number of stitches used gradually dwindled until by the end of the eighteenth century cross stitch was the predominant stitch. Birds, trees, butterflies and animals became more popular subjects, and alphabets and numbers began to appear.

BELOW: Worked in silks on wool tammy, this sampler from 1806 contains alphabets, border patterns, religious verse and motifs, including butterflies and flowers associated with the English garden. (Whitney Antiques)

ABOVE: This charming band sampler, made by 11-year-old Ann Rumgay, is worked in coloured wools with rows of italics and alphabets and small sampler motifs. (Whitney Antiques)

THE INDUSTRIAL REVOLUTION

The Industrial Revolution of the eighteenth century changed the lifestyles of many people in Britain. To begin with, as people moved from the countryside into the towns to work in the new textile mills, there were great hardships. Eventually, as their living standards improved, women from the new middle classes were able to employ domestic help, leaving them with time to pursue crafts which had previously been the privilege of the rich. Crude fancy work and simple embroidery were used to make furnishings such as chair covers, fire screens, footstools and elaborate curtain pelmets, as well as personal items such as prayer book covers, watch pockets and cigar cases.

BERLIN WOOLWORK

Berlin woolwork became fashionable in the early part of the nineteenth century. Introduced from Germany, this cross stitch embroidery on canvas followed a printed pattern and was produced in great abundance by Victorian women. Berlin woolwork did nothing to raise the standard of nineteenth-century embroidery; it did, however, revive the original purpose of the sampler. Typical wool patterns were recorded on scraps of linen or collected together as blocks or motifs grouped on a panel and worked within a decorative border.

ARTS AND CRAFTS MOVEMENT

Following the Great Exhibition of 1851, taste in needlework began to change. Berlin woolwork was seen as gaudy, unimaginative and tedious and groups began to form with the aim of raising the standard of embroidery design and workmanship. Architects and designers such as G. F. Bradley and William Morris were commissioned

ABOVE: An example of Berlin woolwork.

to design embroideries to be worked by groups such as the Ladies' Ecclesiastical Embroidery Society and the Royal School of Art Needlework. The Royal School of Needlework, as it is now known, was founded in 1872 to provide training for young gentlewomen in needlework skills, and to raise the standard of needlecraft design. It soon became quite well known, encouraging the formation of groups in other major cities in Britain. One of the most influential was the Glasgow School, whose work was much inspired by the Scottish Arts and Crafts designer, Charles Rennie Mackintosh. At the Centennial Exposition in 1876, some exhibits from the Royal School of Needlework inspired two influential American designers to set up the Society for Decorative Arts in New York. The founders helped to revitalize and improve the standards in a wide range of crafts throughout the United States of America.

CROSS STITCH KITS

Crochet, knitting and embroidery remained favourite pastimes for women during the 1920s and 30s. Cross stitch kits became popular and transfers were often given away free with magazines.

Fashion changed radically after the Second World War and elaborately embroidered household furnishings were replaced by a minimalistic Scandinavian style. Geometric cross stitch designs and Hardanger work became popular.

EMBROIDERERS' GUILD

Embroidery today owes much of its quality and innovation to the Embroiderers' Guild which was formed in 1920. The group's first president, Louisa Pesel, encouraged members to research historical and ethnic sources in museums. As foreign travel became easier, group members travelled extensively to Asia and Europe, where they were inspired by folk-art embroidery which featured simple traditional stitches such as cross stitch, chain stitch and holbein stitch. During the 1960s art and design became fashionable again and ethnic embroidery was much in demand.

The teaching of needlework skills in schools has unfortunately continued to decline, yet, ironically, the majority of people have more leisure time than ever before. Cross stitch is an easy and rewarding pastime which has increased in popularity over the last twenty years and has the potential to continue to develop as new threads and fabrics become available.

ABOVE LEFT: Fragments of chemise from Mytilini, Greece, late eighteenth century.
ABOVE: A wide variety of stitches have been used in this 1667 sampler, and motifs include "boxer figures" with hair of ravelled silk. (Whitney Antiques)
LEFT: Caucasian/North West Persian cross stitch embroidery, eighteenth century.

ABOVE LEFT: This silk sampler, worked by Caroline Spring in 1824, is a rare English depiction of the crucifixion (Whitney Antiques).
ABOVE RIGHT: A pictorial sampler worked in silks and silk floss by Elizabeth Ross in 1837. Birds, flowers and houses were popular motifs. (Whitney Antiques)
ABOVE: A set of table linen embroidered in England in the late 1940s as a wedding present. LEFT: A wool work sampler from 1850 with an innovative three-dimensional look (Whitney Antiques).

THREADS

Although stranded cotton is probably the most popular and versatile thread for cross stitch embroidery, there is an amazing range of different threads available.

Coton perlé produces attractive raised stitches and tapestry wool makes big, chunky cross stitches on a seven or eight count canvas. Some of the projects in this book use other familiar threads such as coton à broder or soft cotton but many are worked in new threads such as silky Marlitt or the more rustic flower thread which is ideal for stitching on linen. New threads are appearing on the market all the time. Look out for unusual flower threads which have been dyed in shaded natural colours and metallic threads which have been specially made for cross stitching.

FLOWER THREAD OR NORDIN

This rustic cotton thread is ideal for working on evenweave linen fabrics. In thickness it is equivalent to two or three strands of stranded cotton. It is available in solid colours, but look out for the space-dyed skeins.

MARLITT

A lustrous rayon thread, Marlitt has been introduced to provide the sheen and beauty of silk at an economical price. Although only available in solid colours, it has four strands, allowing the colours to be mixed "in the needle".

TAPESTRY WOOL

Although traditionally associated with needlepoint, tapestry wool is also suitable for some cross stitch. It is usually worked on a chunky seven count canvas and makes a warm, hard-wearing cover for cushions, stools and chairs.

COTON PERLÉ

This twisted thread has a distinct pearly sheen and is available in over 300 different colours. It comes in several different thicknesses and is generally used to produce a slightly raised effect on a variety of fabrics.

STRANDED COTTON

This is the most popular embroidery thread and is available in over 400 different colours. It is a versatile thread which can be divided into six separate strands. The separated strands of several colours can be intermingled to create a mottled effect when stitched.

METALLIC THREADS

Although traditionally unsuitable for cross stitch embroidery, some metallic threads are now specially made to sew through fabric. They are available in a range of colours as well as gold and silver. Finer metallic threads known as blending filaments can be worked together with strands of embroidery thread to add an attractive sparkle or sheen.

FABRICS

Evenweave fabrics have the same number of threads running in each direction. The number of threads in each 2½ cm (1 in) of fabric determines the gauge or "count". The larger the number of threads, the finer the fabric. Aida and Hardanger are woven and measured in blocks of threads. However, cross stitches worked on 28 count linen are the same size as those on 14 count Aida because the stitches are worked over two threads of linen.

LINEN

Traditionally pure linen was used, but there are now several different mixed fibre evenweave fabrics in a wide range of colours.

AIDA AND HARDANGER

These popular fabrics have groups of threads woven together to produce distinctive blocks over which the embroidery is worked.

Aida comes in 8–18 count whereas Hardanger is a 22 count fabric. It can be used for fine stitching or worked as an 11 count fabric.

EVENWEAVE BANDS

Aida or evenweave bands come in a variety of widths. Some are plain and others have decorative edges. Once

stitched, these bands can be applied to a background fabric or made up into bows, tie-backs or bags.

FANCY WEAVES

Fabrics specially woven with distinct areas for cross stitching are suitable for making into napkins, tablecloths and cot covers. There are also some unusual evenweaves which have linen or Lurex threads interwoven into the fabric for special effects.

CANVAS

Double and single thread canvas is usually associated with needlepoint but can be used successfully for cross stitch embroidery. Wool and coton perlé are particularly suitable threads for using when stitching on canvas.

WASTE CANVAS

A non-interlocked canvas is used to work cross stitch on non-evenweave fabric or ready-made items. It is specially made so that it can be frayed and removed after the cross stitch is worked.

NON-FRAY FABRICS

Plastic canvas, vinyl weave and stitching paper are all used for cross stitch projects where it is important that the fabric should not fray.

ADDITIONAL FABRICS

Iron-on interfacing is sometimes used to provide a backing for the cross stitch design.

Fusible bonding web is generally used for appliqué.

1: linens; 2: plastic canvas, stitching paper, fusible bonding web, iron-on interfacing; 3: aida and linen bands; 4: 14 and 10 count waste canvas; 5: aida and white Hardanger; 6: canvases; 7: fancy weaves.

TOOLS AND EQUIPMENT

ALL-PURPOSE GLUE

This type of glue is suitable for gluing paper and card (cardboard). Follow the manufacturer's instructions for sticking fabric.

BODKIN/SAFETY PIN

Use either to turn rouleaux or to thread lengths of cord and tape through casings.

COLOURED PENS/PENCILS

Cross stitch charts are much easier to follow if they are coloured in with pencils or pens rather than being drafted in black and white.

COMPASS CUTTER

This specialist tool is ideal for cutting small round shapes from card (cardboard). Protect the work surface with a cutting mat or board.

CRAFT KNIFE

Always use a craft knife with a sharp blade and a safety ruler to cut card safely. Protect the work surface with a cutting mat or board.

DOUBLE-SIDED TAPE

Double-sided tape can be used to stick fabric on to card and mount board (backing board). It is less messy than glue and quicker than using thread.

EASY GRID

These clear acetate sheets with grids printed on them come in different count sizes. They are easy to use and are very useful for creating a cross stitch design from a drawing, photograph or picture.

EASY TURN

This tool makes it easier to turn rouleaux through, but a bodkin or safety pin can be used instead.

EMBROIDERY HOOP (FRAME)

These round frames come in several sizes. A fairly small hoop is ideal for most designs stitched on linen-type fabrics as the frame can be moved as you work. Always release the fabric from the hoop at the end of each sewing session. Embroidery hoops are unsuitable for canvas work as the tight rings damage the canvas.

FRAME

Cross stitch projects are usually worked in a frame. The frame holds the material firm so the stitches remain even and accurately spaced. Each project has a recommended frame, but there are many different frames available for cross stitching and you may have a personal preference for one type.

GRAPH PAPER

This paper is used to draft cross stitch charts and is generally marked out in blocks of 10 squares for easy counting. It is available in other counts to work out a design to the actual size it appears on the fabric.

HOLE PUNCH

This type of hole punch cuts one hole at a time and is more versatile for craft projects.

INTERLOCKING BAR FRAME

These bars are sold in pairs and can be made to fit any size of project but are especially useful for working small square or rectangular projects. The fabric is stretched and temporarily pinned or stapled to the frame until the work is complete.

MASKING TAPE

This tape is useful for temporary sticking. It can be used to prevent evenweave fabric fraying or used to hold wood or card (cardboard) together while the glue dries.

NEEDLES

Tapestry needles have a large eye to accommodate the thicker embroidery thread and a blunt point to prevent the fabric threads being damaged. They come in various graded sizes from fine (14) to coarse (26).

Embroidery (crewel) needles are similar to tapestry needles but have a sharp point.

PAINTBRUSHES

Use good quality brushes for painting, matching the type and size of the brush to the project. Sponge or poly brushes are ideal for applying emulsion-type paints. They do not leave brush marks and make it fairly easy to paint a straight edge.

PROJECT CARD

Thread sorters can be made from plastic or card (cardboard). They hold cut lengths of thread, in each colour, ready to use in the project.

QUILTER'S PENCIL

Use this special pencil to make fine marks or guidelines on fabric which can be washed. Silver shows up well on dark fabrics and yellow is ideal for lighter colours.

ROTARY FRAME

This frame is used mainly for canvas work or long pieces of work such as band samplers and bell pulls. Each end of the evenweave fabric is stitched securely to the webbing of the frame and then rolled up until the fabric is taut.

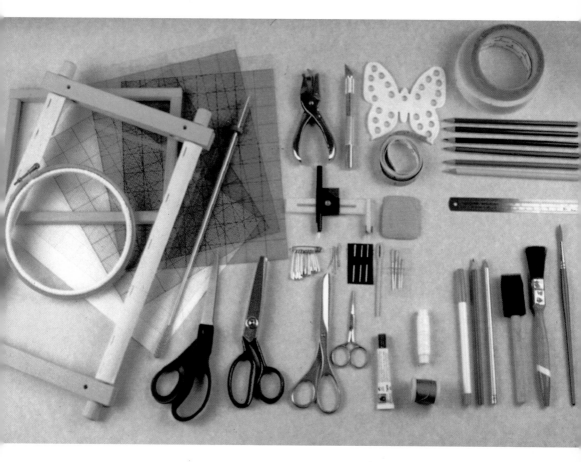

SCISSORS

Keep separate scissors for cutting paper and for fabric, and choose different scissors depending on the size of the work involved. Small embroidery scissors are ideal for snipping threads while larger scissors should be used to cut pieces of fabric. Pinking shears are used to cut a serrated, decorative edge on fabric making it less likely to fray.

TAILOR'S CHALK

This is used to make a temporary rough mark or line on fabric before cutting or stitching.

TAPE MEASURE/RULER

Use a tape to measure fabric and a ruler for paper and card (cardboard). Always remember that special safety rulers are recommended when cutting card with a craft knife.

THREADS

Although tacking (basting) thread is generally white and breaks more easily than sewing thread, use any contrasting colour thread for tacking and marking guidelines on evenweave fabrics. When stitching and making up the projects use a matching sewing thread.

TOP ROW: rotary frame, embroidery hoop (frame), interlocking bar frame, graph paper, Easy grid, easy turn, hole punch, craft knife, project card, tape measure, double-sided tape, masking tape, coloured pencils. SECOND ROW: compass cutter, tailor's chalk, ruler. THIRD ROW: safety pins, pins, needles, bodkin, tapestry needles. BOTTOM ROW: dressmaking scissors, pinking shears, paper scissors, embroidery scissors, all-purpose glue, white tacking (basting) thread, sewing thread, vanishing ink pen, pencil, quilting pencil, poly brush, paintbrushes.

VANISHING INK PEN

The ink from this pen vanishes completely after several days and is ideal to use if the project will not be washed after making up.

BASIC STITCHES

Cross stitch can either be worked as a single stitch or in a row which is completed in two journeys. Irrespective of which method is used, the top stitch should always face in the same direction. If working a border or a detailed piece of cross stitch, it is helpful to put a pin in the work showing the direction in which the top stitch should face.

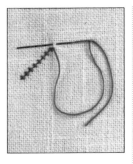

SINGLE CROSS STITCH

This produces a slightly raised cross and should be used for individual stitches and small details. It is also ideal when stitching with tapestry wool.

SMYRNA CROSS STITCH

This decorative stitch is made up of a single cross stitch with an upright cross worked on top. It can be worked in one colour or two colours.

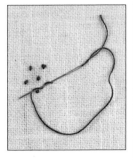

FRENCH KNOT

The French knot is a raised stitch used to add tiny details, such as eyes, flower centres and berries or to add texture to large areas of cross stitch.

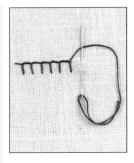

BLANKET STITCH

Use this stitch to neaten the edges of evenweave fabric before working the cross stitch design or decorative edging on mats, waistcoats and bags.

ROW OF CROSS STITCH

First work a row of half cross stitches either diagonally or in a straight line. Complete the cross stitches by stitching the other half on the way back.

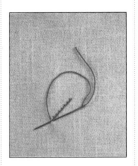

THREE-QUARTER CROSS STITCH

This stitch is used when more detail and precise colour changes are required. It is made up of a half and quarter cross stitch.

RUNNING STITCH

This is used for tacking (basting) guidelines and stitching decorative details Holbein stitch is similar but the spaces are filled in with a second row.

BACKSTITCH

This produces a slightly raised linear stitch. It is used to work lines and to outline areas of cross stitch. The surface stitches are the same length.

WORKING FROM A CHART

The cross stitch charts in this book are made up of coloured blocks with symbols and straight lines. The symbols allow you to photocopy the chart and enlarge it if required. Each coloured square represents one cross stitch and the straight lines are backstitch.

Every project has detailed instructions telling you how to mark the exact position of the cross stitch and where to begin. Usually there are two guidelines running across the middle of the fabric in both directions. It may help, especially on larger projects, to tack (baste) the guidelines carefully, going over and under ten threads at a time. The cross stitch is then worked from the centre outwards.

The size of the stitch is determined by the type of fabric and threads used in the project. Some fabrics, like Aida and Hardanger, are woven in fabric blocks to make counting and stitching fairly straightforward. Evenweave fabrics, such as linen and Jobelan, on the other hand, are worked over a number of threads. Do not be daunted by the prospect of working on linen-type fabrics. They may appear more difficult to work on but, in fact, they are much easier than they look and the results are worth the extra effort.

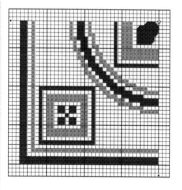

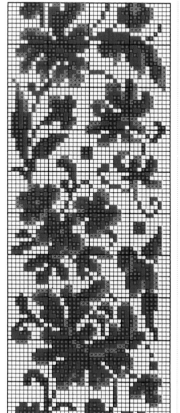

WORKING A REPEAT

Sometimes, because of restrictions in space, only part of the chart is shown. Shelf or curtain border charts, for example, show a single motif or a block which can be repeated. The project instructions explain exactly where to stitch the next motif. If it is a repeat pattern, continue the design, block by block as far as required.

WORKING A QUARTER CHART

Read the instructions carefully and look at the finished project before completing a quarter chart. The final appearance of the cross stitch will depend on how you repeat the design. The work can be done in any one of the three following ways:

1 Stitch one quarter, work the mirror image of this first quarter in the next space and complete the design by working the mirror image of the completed first half. (Work out the mirror image by holding a mirror along one edge of the chart and transferring the reversed image to a piece of graph paper.)

2 Mark the evenweave into four equal squares and stitch the same motif in each area.

3 Stitch one quarter, turn the fabric through 90 degrees and work the same design again. Repeat another two times to complete the embroidery.

TECHNIQUES:BEGINNING

PREPARING THE FABRIC

Many of the projects in this book use evenweave fabrics which tend to fray easily, therefore it is advisable to finish the edges before starting the embroidery. An allowance has been made for neatening the edges in calculating the materials needed.

MASKING TAPE

A quick method for projects worked on inter-locking bar frames. The tape can be stapled or pinned to a frame.

ZIGZAG

Machine-stitched zigzag is used when embroidering parts of a garment since the seams will be neatened ready to stitch together.

BLANKET STITCH

This is the best all round method of neatening evenweave fabric. Either turn a small hem or stitch round the raw edge.

LEFT TO RIGHT: masking tape, zigzag and blanket stitch.

COVERING A HOOP

Embroidery hoops (frames) have two rings, one is solid and the other has a screw-fastening. The fabric is sandwiched between the two rings and the screw-fastening adjusted to keep the fabric taut. In order to protect the fabric and stitches from damage, the inner ring is wrapped with narrow cotton tape. Remember that some delicate fabrics can be damaged in an embroidery hoop (frame). In these cases it is advisable to use a large hoop which extends beyond the cross stitch area. Interlocking bar frames are ideal for small projects and a rotating frame is best for large pieces of work.

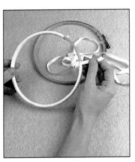

STARTING & FINISHING THREADS

There are several ways to begin a piece of cross stitch. Finish by sliding the needle under several stitches and trimming the end.

1 Fold a length of cotton in half and thread into the needle. Work the first half of the cross stitch, then thread the needle through the loop on the reverse side.

2 Leave a length of 5 cm (2 in) thread at the back of the fabric and weave this in when you have worked a block of stitches.

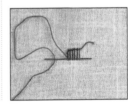

WASTE CANVAS

This technique allows charted cross stitch to be worked on non-evenweave fabric or ready-made items such as towels and cushions. Waste canvas is specially made so that the threads can be easily removed. It is only available in 10 and 14 count but you could use ordinary canvas provided that the threads are not interlocked.

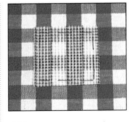

1 Tack (baste) a piece of canvas onto the area to be stitched. Make sure there will be plenty of canvas round the design once it is complete.

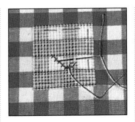

2 Work the cross stitch design over the canvas and through the fabric. Take care to make all the stitches as even as you possibly can.

3 Once complete, fray the canvas and pull the threads out one at a time. It will be easier if you tug the canvas gently to loosen the threads.

TECHNIQUES: FINISHING

MITRED CORNER

Tablecloths and mats can be finished neatly with mitred corners. These reduce bulk and make a secure hem which can be laundered safely.

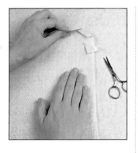 

1 Fold the hem, run your fingers along and open out. Cut across the corner from crease to crease and refold the hem.

2 Turn under a further 0.5 cm (¼ in) and pin the hem in place. Slip stitch the mitred corner and machine or hand stitch the hem.

STRETCHING

As a general rule embroidery should always be stretched using thread so that it can be easily removed and cleaned in the future. However, small projects which may be kept for only a limited time can be quickly and successfully mounted using double-sided tape.

1 Cut the card (cardboard) to the required size and stick double-sided tape along all the edges. Trim across the corners and remove the paper backing. Stretch the fabric onto the tape and mitre the corners neatly.

MOUNTING

If a project such as a sampler or picture is likely to be kept for a long time, great care should be taken in mounting the finished work. Acid-free mount board (backing board) or paper should be used under the embroidery and glue or tape which leave an acid residue on the fabric should be avoided.

The following easy method of mounting ensures that the embroidery will be absolutely straight and exactly where you want it.

1 Cut the mount board to size and mark the mid point across the top and bottom of the board. Allow for a wider border at the bottom if required. Mark the mid point of the embroidery at each side of the board and draw in the lines. Lay the embroidery face down on a flat surface and place the mount board on top of it.

2 Line up the guide-lines on the embroidery with the lines on the board. Fold the top edge over and put a pin into the mount board at the centre line. Stretch the fabric slightly and put another pin at the bottom. Repeat the process at the sides. Work your way along each edge from the centre out putting in pins every 2.5 cm (1 in) keeping the grain of the fabric straight.

3 Using a long length of double thread, sew from side to side spacing the stitches about 12 mm (½ in) apart. Join in more thread using an overhand knot. Once complete lift the threads up one at a time to pull them tight and secure. Mitre or fold the corners and repeat along the remaining sides.

ADDITIONS

Most embroidery is embellished by the addition of trimmings, and cross stitch is no exception. Whether it is an Asian design with shisha mirrors and tassels or a traditional English lavender bag edged with Victorian lace, the "additions" always enhance the cross stitch design and add the finishing touch to an attractive piece.

BEADS

Beads are attached using a double thread and in contrast to all other forms of embroidery, begun with a securely tied knot. Sew the beads on individually, as if you were stitching the first half of a cross stitch.

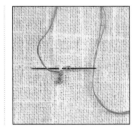

BUTTONS

Buttons with four holes can be stitched on with a large cross stitch to make a very attractive addition to a design.

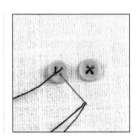

RIBBON

Ribbon looks very effective when used to create a grid for a repeat design of small cross stitch motifs. The ribbon is laid straight along the grain before the cross stitch has been worked. Choose a ribbon which is the same width as one cross stitch. If the ribbon is to be applied diagonally it is easier to work the cross stitch motifs first.

1 Pin the strips of ribbon in position in one direction and pin the rest across the top. Check that the spacing is correct, then tack the ends.

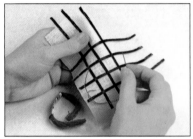

2 Sew a cross stitch at each junction where the ribbons overlap. Remember that if the ribbons are applied diagonally, the cross stitch will be upright.

MAKING A CORD

Embroidery threads are ideal for making into fine cord. The threads can be all one colour or mixed colours to match each particular project.

The amount of thread you need depends on the final thickness of the cord required. As a rough guide, a 1 m (39 in) length of threads ready to twist will make a cord about 40 cm (16 in) long.

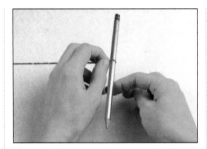

1 Cut several lengths of thread, two and a half times the final cord length. Fix one end to a secure point. Slip a pencil through the threads at the other end and twist the pencil like a propeller.

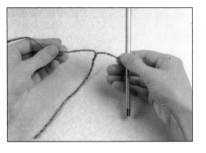

2 Keep turning until the cord begins to twist together. Hold the middle of the cord and bring the ends together. Smooth any kinks with your fingers and tie the ends with an overhand knot.

SHISHA MIRROR

These irregular pieces of mirror are stitched on to garments and hangings as a protection against evil. If spirits see themselves reflected in the mirror then, it is believed, they will flee.

Traditional shisha mirrors can be bought from ethnic suppliers, but large modern sequins are a suitable alternative. As extra security, stick the mirror or sequins in position using a small piece of double-sided tape or a dab of glue.

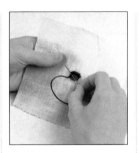

1 Sew two threads across the shisha from top to bottom. Sew across the shisha in the other direction looping the thread round each laid thread to create a framework.

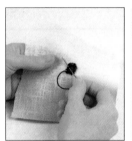

2 Bring the needle up close to the shisha, make a loop through the framework, cross over the loop and pull the thread gently towards you. Take the needle back to the reverse side.

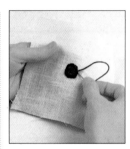

3 Continue round the shisha beginning each stitch between the ends of the previous loop. Finish the thread off on the reverse side.

MAKING TASSELS

One of the prettiest ways to complete a project is to make your own tassels from threads which were used in the embroidery. There are many different ways to make tassels, but most use the same basic technique.

The two following methods are both easy to make. The first tassel is ideal for stitching on to the corners of cushions, mats or bookmarks whereas the second is worked over the end of a cord or rouleau and produces a very professional result. Make the tassels more ornate by adding beads or stitching rows of interlocking blanket stitch round the head until it is completely covered.

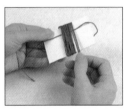

1 Cut a piece of card (cardboard) slightly deeper than the finished length of the tassel. Wind threads round the card as required and slip a length of thread underneath.

2 Cut along the bottom of the threads and tie the bundle together using a sailor's knot. This is like a reef knot, but the thread is twisted round twice before pulling it tight.

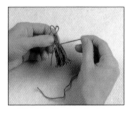

3 Wrap another length of thread round the tassel to form a neck and tie off as before. Trim the ends neatly.

1 Wind threads round the card (cardboard) and cut along one side. Tie a knot near the end of the cord or rouleau and place it in the middle of the bundle of threads.

2 Enclose the knot with the threads and tie a separate length of thread around just above the knot.

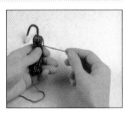

3 Hold the cord and bring all the threads down together. Wrap a length of cord round underneath the knot and tie off securely as before. Trim the tassel ends neatly.

MAKING BIAS STRIPS

Bias strips, cut across the diagonal grain of fabric, are useful for binding edges, making piping and making into rouleaux. The strips stretch lengthways and widthways, making it easy to fit the piping or binding round corners.

1 Fold one corner of the fabric over till the selvedge meets the straight grain and press down the fold. Using tailor's chalk, draw lines across the fabric parallel to the fold line. The width of the strips will depend on the project, but they are usually 5–8 cm (2–3 in) wide.

2 Bias strips are joined together by stitching along the straight grain. Pin two pieces together as shown and stitch. If there is an obvious right and wrong side to the fabric, one end of the strip may have to be trimmed. Press the seam flat and trim the points of fabric which are sticking out.

MAKING ROULEAUX

A rouleau is literally "a roll of fabric". It is made from a strip of bias fabric which has been folded lengthways and stitched. The seam allowance forms the padding when the strip is turned through. Rouleaux can be used as a drawstring instead of cord, they can be stitched on to cross stitch designs in the same way as ribbon to create texture or plaited together to make a bag strap.

1 Press a 5 cm (2 in) bias strip to remove some of the stretch. Fold the strip lengthways and stitch 8 mm (5/16 in) from the folded edge. Trim the raw edge and feed the tube on to an easy turn rouleau maker.

ABOVE: Rouleaux can be used to add an attractive three-dimensional element to ethnic and contemporary cross stitch designs.

2 Hook the wire on to the end of the fabric tube and pull gently to turn the rouleau through.

This is by far the easiest way to make rouleaux but you can use a large needle or bodkin instead. For a more padded effect, pull strands of wool through the rouleau as it is being turned or thread through later with a large needle.

FINISHING A CUSHION

Cushions come in all shapes and sizes. Small cushions filled with pot pourri or herbs look most attractive with a lace or wide ribbon frill whereas larger cushions can be given a professional finish with a piped edge.

TO EDGE WITH LACE

1 Measure the perimeter of the cushion and cut a piece of lace twice that length. Sew two rows of gathering threads along the straight edge of the lace. Gather the lace up to fit the perimeter of the cushion and pin it in place. Adjust the gathers and tack (baste). To join the ends of the lace, trim round a motif, overlap the ends and hand stitch securely.

TO PIPE THE EDGES

1 Cut and join enough bias strips to fit round the outside of the cushion. Fold the bias strip over the piping cord with the right side facing out, and then tack (baste) close to the cord.

2 Pin and tack the piping along the seam line. Either overlap the ends or mark the length of piping required and sew the bias strip together before tacking (basting) the last edge.

One of the embroidery thread colours has been picked out and used for the contrasting piped edge on this pretty cushion.

COVERING A FRAME

Picture frames, photo mounts and mirror frames are all begun in the same way. The technique of covering card (cardboard) mounts with fabric has become much easier with the introduction of double-sided tape.

1 Cut the mount board (backing board) to size and draw the position of the opening. It is usual for the borders to be equal at the top and sides and slightly deeper along the bottom. Cut out the middle of the mount.

2 Lay the embroidered panel face down and place the mount on top. Cut into the corners and trim the fabric to about 1.5 cm (⅝ in). Stick double-sided tape along the inner edge of the mount then stick the fabric flaps on to the tape. Keep the fabric straight along the edge of the mount. Mitre the outside corners and stick the remaining fabric on to the board. The mount can be stitched onto backing card and made into a frame.

INSPIRATION

This book is not only about working and experimenting with the wide variety of threads and fabrics available today, but also aims to inspire you, as you gain in confidence, to create your own designs for cross stitch projects.

There are many different approaches to designing but initially you must find a source of inspiration. You can draw, paint or photograph natural forms such as a collection of shells and pebbles found on the beach, a bowl of brightly coloured fruit or a vase of flowers. Man-made objects, buildings for example, are often forgotten, but look for interesting features on doors, reflections in a window or unusual tile patterns on the floor. Build up a collection of sketches and photographs of things which you find interesting. Don't worry if you are not inspired immediately - often the best work comes from a seemingly insignificant sketch or detail recorded which is developed only at a later date.

ABOVE: A collection of pieces such as these from India and Pakistan offer a wealth of ideas.
RIGHT: Make your own collection of cards, gift wrap and fabrics and use for inspiration.

As well as working from the things that surround us, you may also be inspired by an image or an object made by someone else. Art galleries and museums are rich sources of work by other artists from all over the world. As well as drawings and paintings there are weavings, clothes, pottery and other artefacts which might be of interest.

You could copy a piece of work and produce a design in the style of that artist or use an element of the artist's work in a personal and creative way.

Traditional crafts are another rich source of ideas. Craftsmen throughout history have made objects and embellished them in a way that goes far beyond their functional use. These people did not necessarily draw or paint their designs first, they were inspired by the colours and the landscape around them and worked innovatively using the basic colours and materials available.

The main difficulty people have when they want to create their own designs is taking a three-dimensional object and getting it down on paper in a two-dimensional form. Many people think that they are not artistic and lack the confidence to draw or paint designs from real life. Remember that it is quite possible to produce designs from other sources such as books, magazines, cards, gift wrap or photographs. These images are already in two dimensions and can be used immediately in your design.

Detailed sketches of unusual artefacts, such as these beautiful pots, may be developed at a later date into a cross stitch design.

EXPERIMENTING

EXPERIMENTING WITH THREADS

Cross stitch is a simple stitch which can be used to create very intricate designs using a wide spectrum of colours. Sometimes in order to

1 Colour mix threads by stitching the first half of the stitch in one colour and the second half in another. This technique is used quite extensively in Indian textiles and looks most effective on coloured linen or painted canvas.

Find out how many different combinations there are using the original four contrasting colours. There will be a subtle change if the threads are swapped around and the bottom colour is on the top and vice versa.

Some of the thread combinations produce dark colours but others are much brighter and lighter.

reduce the range of colours required or make a subtle change from one colour to the next, different threads can be mixed on the same stitch.

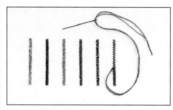

2 Alternatively, mix the colours "in the needle". Put two or three different coloured threads in the needle and work the cross stitch as normal.

Experiment with bands of light and dark thread combinations to create a three-dimensional effect on a striped border design.

This technique also works well if the cross stitch is worked diagonally using conventional or upright cross stitch. Introduce a change of texture by combining the two types of cross

stitch together. Smyrna stitch is often worked in two different colours. Work the conventional cross stitch in one colour and stitch an upright cross stitch over it using a contrasting colour.

EXPERIMENTING WITH FABRIC

Traditionally single canvas is used for needlepoint designs where the entire canvas is covered in tent stitch (half cross stitch). When using cross stitch twice as much thread or yarn goes into each hole of the fabric, it is therefore essential that you choose a canvas with a larger count than you would for needlepoint. For example, traditional needlepoint is worked using tapestry wool on 10 count canvas, but wool cross stitch needs a 7 or 8 count canvas.

Experiment using other yarns on

different counts of canvas. Canvas tends to be white or beige and is not designed to be seen but it can be painted or dyed successfully. Spray paint, including car paint, is ideal for colouring the canvas. All types of fabric dye can also be used.

Interlocked canvas will not fray and it can therefore be cut into squares before stitching. Small motifs stitched on painted canvas look very effective mounted on handmade paper or stitched on to a contrasting fabric background.

Sponge the dye onto both sides of the canvas and allow to dry thoroughly before stitching.

EXPERIMENTING WITH CHARTS

Cross stitch charts can be interpreted in different ways. When working on Hardanger, linen or other evenweave fabrics the shape and size of a design can be altered quite easily. Try experimenting with a simple heart motif.

CHANGING THE DIMENSIONS

1 Stitch a tiny motif such as this, using a single strand of cotton over one thread of linen. Work the same motif on a larger scale using two strands of cotton over two threads.

2 Lengthen the heart motif by working over two threads horizontally and three threads down. Make the motif wider by stitching across three threads instead of two.

RIGHT: This heart motif has been stitched in Nordin on 28 count linen, on a 10 count canvas using coton perlé no. 5 and finally in tapestry wool on a 7 count canvas.

CHANGING THE SCALE

A charted design can also be worked using different threads and fabric to create the same design on a different scale. In this way you use some of the cross stitch designs in this book on other similar items, you can also make a range of matching projects using the same designs on different scales.

EXPERIMENTING WITH LETTERS

Letters have been used throughout history as form of decoration, from illuminated manuscipts to household linen. Choose one of the many alphabets available for cross stitchers today and personalize it using this simple technique.

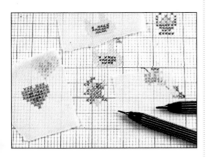

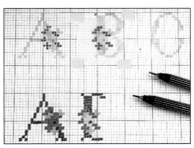

1 Draw some small motifs which you would like to incorporate with the letters. Lay pieces of tracing paper over the design motifs and copy using coloured pens or pencils.

2 Copy some letters on to graph paper and place a traced motif on top. Move the motif around until it is in a satisfactory position. Once you are happy with the arrangement, tape the motif in position and copy the decorated letter onto graph paper. Repeat the process with other letters and experiment with different motifs.

❖ ❖ ❖ ❖ ❖
NEEDLEWORK TIP

Monograms, which are groups of two or more letters, can be easily designed and created using the same technique. Draw out the letters for the monogram on graph paper. Trace one of the letters and move it over the other letter till you find an attractive arrangement. Tape the tracing paper in position and draw the monogram overlapping or intertwining the letters as required.

TRACING & TRANSFERRING

Nowadays, with the right computer equipment, it is possible to scan pictures directly into a cross stitch or graphics program and produce your own charts. The design can be simplified on screen by merging colours to reduce the number of different colours needed. Colours can be changed readily and interesting details, borders or motifs can be copied and used to create new attractive designs.

Most of us though, still need to transfer a design onto graph paper to create a chart for cross stitch. You can draw directly onto graph paper, but the finished design can look "boxy". It is possible to trace and transfer a simple motif but the simplest method is to use an "Easy grid." This is a sheet of clear acetate which has been printed with grid lines. The grids come in different sizes to match the various counts of fabric. You can also use a colour photocopier to enlarge or reduce the design before using the correct count grid to make the chart.

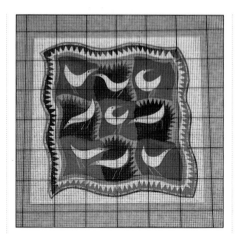

1 Choose a picture which is the same size as the finished cross stitch. Lay the selected grid on top of the picture and tape down. Either work the cross stitch directly from the grid or transfer the design onto graph paper. If a square is mainly one colour then stitch it that colour. If the square is half and half, work two three-quarter cross stitches, one in each colour to fill the square.

NEEDLEWORK TIP

If the picture you want to use is larger or smaller than the proposed size of cross stitch, you can use a different count Easy grid to scale the chart up or down. For example, you might want a 40 cm (16 in) square cross stitch design for a cushion using tapestry wool on 7 count canvas, but the picture you have is only 20 cm (8 in) square. In this case use a 14 count Easy grid to make a chart from the picture and the design will work out the correct size.

TO TRACE THE DESIGN

If the picture you wish to use is much smaller than the finished size of the proposed cross stitch, it is often quicker to trace and enlarge the design using squared paper. Remember that the final result you achieve will depend upon how accurately you trace the initial picture. When tracing, always use a very sharp hard pencil and take care to draw the details exactly.

1 Lay the tracing paper over the picture area and secure with masking tape. Draw round the edges of the design motif carefully with a sharp pencil. Try to include as many of the tiny details as possible to make the enlarged design more accurate and interesting.

2 Turn the tracing paper over onto the graph paper and position the design . Draw along the lines carefully. In this way the design will be inverted. To reproduce the original motif, scribble over the reverse side of the tracing and then draw over the lines.

TO ENLARGE THE DESIGN

1 Draw a line round the design area and adapt the motif to suit. In this case, a stem has been added to the flower head.

Draw a similarly shaped large rectangle the exact size of the proposed cross stitch design. Count the squares across and down the side of the small motif and then mark out the same number on the larger grid. Working from left to right, square by square transfer the lines from the small to the larger grid.

Above: Once you have transferred a design you can use it as a small detail, or a large, bold, single motif, as on this cushion.

2 Refer to the original picture and mark the shaded areas on the petals and flower centre. Use pens or pencils to colour the design. The design can be worked directly from the graph paper using 10 count waste canvas or use the appropriate sheet of Easy grid to stitch on other counts of evenweave fabric.

TO ROTATE THE DESIGN

At this stage, the design could be transferred onto computer. There are many cross stitch design packages now available which allow you greater flexibility and speed when trying out different colourways of the same design. Cross stitch computer programs also enable you to flip motifs vertically and horizontally as well as rotating them through 45 or 90 degrees. This feature is invaluable when designing borders and turning corners. If you do not have access to a computer the traditional method of rotating, using a mirror is quite satisfactory.

1 Stand a mirror tile upright on the cross stitch chart at an angle of 45 degrees. On a separate piece of graph paper draw out the corner design you can see reflected in the mirror. To get a mirror image, hold the mirror straight along the edge of the cross stitch motif and draw the reversed image.

TEMPLATES

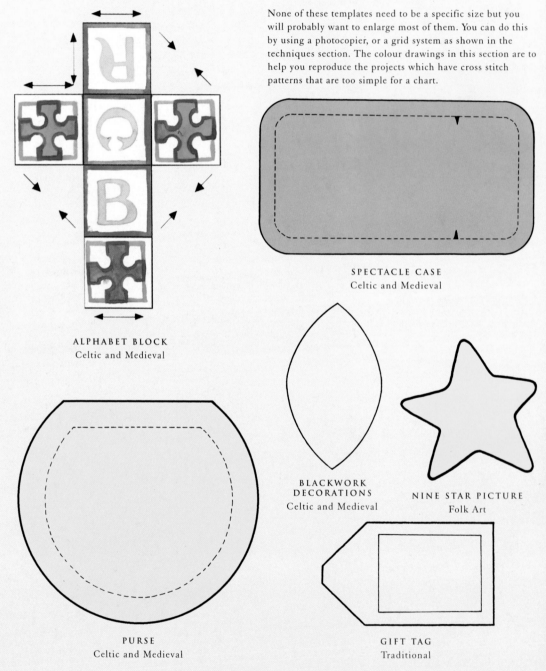

None of these templates need to be a specific size but you will probably want to enlarge most of them. You can do this by using a photocopier, or a grid system as shown in the techniques section. The colour drawings in this section are to help you reproduce the projects which have cross stitch patterns that are too simple for a chart.

ALPHABET BLOCK
Celtic and Medieval

SPECTACLE CASE
Celtic and Medieval

BLACKWORK DECORATIONS
Celtic and Medieval

NINE STAR PICTURE
Folk Art

PURSE
Celtic and Medieval

GIFT TAG
Traditional

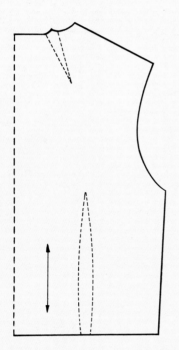

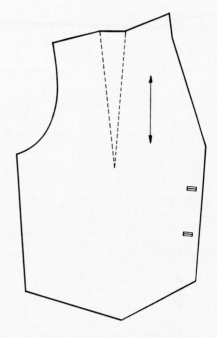

WAISTCOAT
Celtic and Medieval

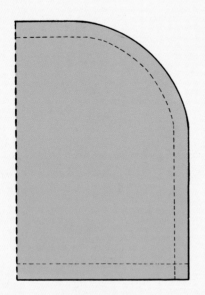

**COTTAGE GARDEN
TEA COSY**

Traditional

EMBROIDERED BOOK
Contemporary

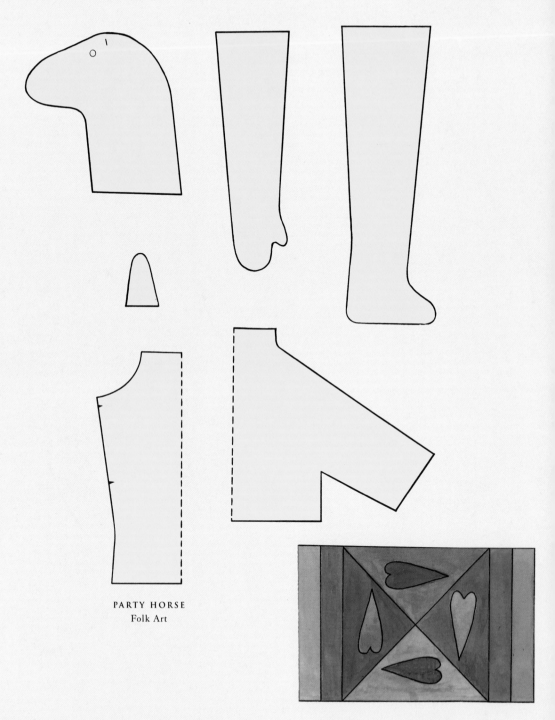

PARTY HORSE
Folk Art

TRAY CLOTH
Folk Art

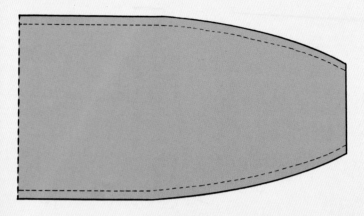

TIE BACKS
Contemporary

GARDEN APRON
Contemporary

CHILD'S WAISTCOAT
Contemporary

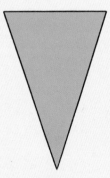

**TRADITIONAL
CHRISTMAS STOCKING**
Traditional

**VICTORIAN
SCISSORS CASE**
Traditional

CHILD'S BAG
Contemporary

CHAPTER ONE

CELTIC AND MEDIEVAL

Capture the excitement and colour of medieval
pageants, festivals and lavish tournaments
with the designs in this section. Choose
from intricate knot work designs from ornately
carved Celtic masonry or the bold and
colourful embroidery inspired by exquisitely
detailed illuminated manuscripts,
and the beautiful stained-glass windows
found in churches and monasteries
in the Middle Ages.

MEDIEVAL TIEBACKS

*These beautiful chunky tiebacks are the ideal size to hold back
a big heavy curtain for the front door.*

YOU WILL NEED

*70 cm (³⁄₄ yd) natural
hessian fabric*

scissors

pins

tacking (basting) thread

needle

*tapestry wool Anchor two
10 m skeins of 8400, four of
8592 and five of 8630*

tapestry needle

embroidery hoop (frame)

70 cm (³⁄₄ yd) lining fabric

70 cm (³⁄₄ yd) wadding (batting)

sewing thread

two large brass curtain rings

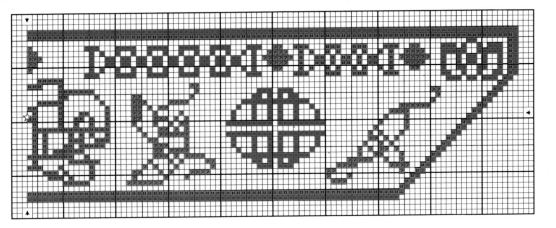

WORKING THE CROSS STITCH

The size of these tiebacks will depend very much on the type of hessian you buy. You can adjust the size to match the curtains. Mark off 20 threads in each direction with pins and measure. This will be equivalent to 10 squares on the chart. Work out the length and depth required and add extra for fringing. Cut a piece of hessian the required size. Tack (baste) guidelines in both directions across the hessian and work the cross stitch over two threads. Once complete, press on the wrong side and trim to 12 mm (½ in).

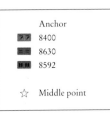

Anchor	
77	8400
▄▄	8630
▓▓	8592
☆	Middle point

1 To make up: cut the lining fabric the same size and fold under a 12 mm (½ in) seam allowance. Cut a piece of wadding (batting) slightly smaller than the pressed lining. Lay the tieback face down and put the wadding on top. Pin the lining through all the layers and hem close to the cross stitch.

2 Sew a curtain ring on the inside at each end of the tieback. Make a fringe by carefully fraying the hessian with a blunt needle as far up as the stitching. Make a second tieback in the same way, if required.

MEDIEVAL CUSHION

Young teenagers will love the bright colours and bold heraldic patterns
in this design. The cushion is the ideal size for lounging on a bed.

YOU WILL NEED

46 cm (18 in) square of
7 count Sudan canvas

needle

tacking (basting) thread

tapestry wool Anchor
8004, 8016, 8114, 8140, 8218,
8414, 8588, 8714, 8788, 8784,
9078, 9096, 9768

tapestry needle

rotating frame

pins

scissors

180 cm (2 yd) natural cord
piping

sewing thread

sewing machine

46 x 56 cm (18 x 22 in)
cream backing fabric

40 cm (16 in) cushion pad

WORKING
THE CROSS STITCH

Tack (baste) guidelines
across the centre of the
canvas in both direc-
tions. Work the cross
stitch and once it is
completed, block to even
out the stitches and
square up the design.

1 To make up: tack (baste) the piping
round the edge of the cross stitch and
machine in place. Stitch a 1 cm (³⁄₈ in) hem
on both short ends of the backing fabric. Cut
crossways down the centre and overlap the
hems to make a 30 cm (12 in) square.

2 Tack the backing pieces together and pin
on top of the cross stitch with right sides
facing. Tack and machine round the sides.

3 Trim the seams and cut across the
corners before turning through. Press
lightly and insert the cushion pad.

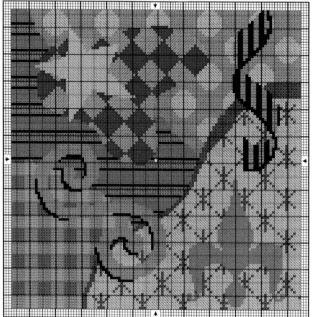

	Anchor		Anchor		Anchor
═ ═	8588	⋉ ⋉	9078	△ △	8114
⤬ ⤬	8414	╲ ╲	8016	∧ ∧	8140
⤫ ⤫	8004	▰ ▰	9768	⤬ ⤬	8788
╱ ╱	8714	○ ○	9096	☆	Middle
и и	8784	⊬ ⊬	8218		point

CELTIC CUSHION

This cushion will look most effective teamed with several others in different shades of blue and yellow and scattered on a couch.

YOU WILL NEED

35 cm (14 in) square of 7 count Sudan canvas

tacking (basting) thread

needle

tapestry wool Anchor 8 skeins of 8704, 4 skeins of 8896, 2 skeins each of 8020 & 8836

tapestry needle

rotating frame

pins

scissors

125 cm (1¹⁄₃ yd) blue cord piping

sewing thread

sewing machine

30 x 38 cm (12 x 15 in) deep blue backing fabric

30 cm (12 in) cushion pad

WORKING THE CROSS STITCH

Tack (baste) guidelines across the centre of the canvas in both directions. Work the cross stitch and block once completed to even out the stitches and square up the design.

1 To make up: tack (baste) the piping round the edge of the cross stitch and machine in place. Stitch a 1 cm (³⁄₈ in) hem on both short ends of the backing fabric. Cut crossways down the centre and overlap the hems to make a 30 cm (12 in) square. Tack (baste) the backing pieces together and pin on top of the cross stitch with right sides facing.

2 Tack round all the sides and machine. Trim the seams and cut across the corners before turning through. Press lightly and insert the cushion pad.

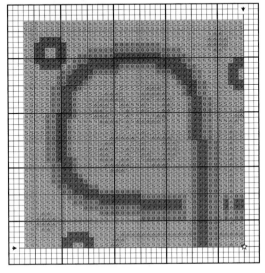

	Anchor		Anchor		
5 5	8704	7 7	8836	☆	Middle point
6 6	8020	8 8	8896		

FIREGUARD

Fitted into a fireguard, this fantastic dragon design makes a
wonderful screen in front of an empty fire.

YOU WILL NEED

tacking (basting) thread

needle

51 x 61 cm (20 x 24 in)
grey/blue 28 count Quaker
evenweave linen

stranded cotton Anchor two
skeins of 1014 and 891

one skein of 273, 274, 357, 403,
779, 830, 831, 849, 853, 855,
856, 868, 875, 877, 898, 900,
943, 945, 5975, 8581

tapestry needle

embroidery hoop (frame)

mount board (backing board)

craft knife

safety ruler

strong thread

fireguard

WORKING THE CROSS STITCH

Although this is a large project, it is sewn on
evenweave linen and it can be worked a small
area at a time, in a small round embroidery
frame to make it easier to handle.

1 Tack (baste) guidelines across middle of the
linen in both directions and work the cross
stitch over two threads using two strands of
cotton. Work the backstitch on the wings using a
single strand of 900 and all other backstitch using
two strands of 403.

2 To make up: press the embroidery on the
reverse side. Cut the mount board (backing
board) to fit the fireguard. Stretch the embroidery
over the mount board and fit into the fireguard.

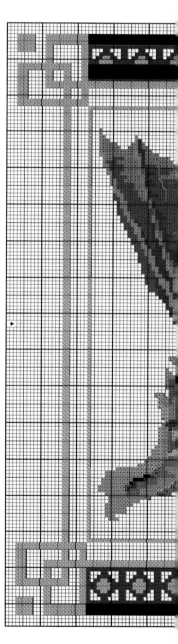

	Anchor		Anchor		Anchor		Anchor		Anchor
	357		856		945		403		868/5975
	830		891		1014		274/875		849/877
	831		898		5975		779/877		853/855
	853		900		8581		830/943		831/898
	855		943		273		830/831		898/945

☆ Middle point

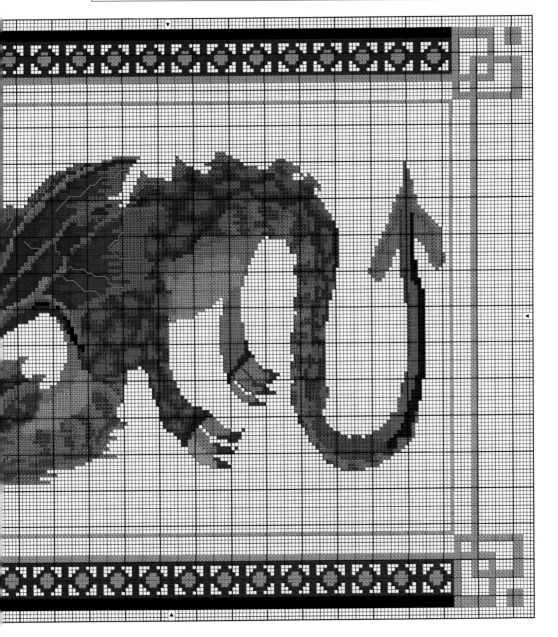

NAPKIN RING

*These unusual napkin rings will look very elegant
slipped around plain linen napkins.*

YOU WILL NEED

*5 x 15 cm (2 x 6 in)
10 count single canvas*

tapestry needle

stranded cotton Anchor 70, 276

scissors

5 x 15 cm (2 x 6 in) cream felt

needle

WORKING THE CROSS STITCH

Work the design using all six
strands of cotton. The stitches
will lie better if you separate the
strands and put them together
again before sewing. Press the
embroidery on the wrong side
once completed.

1 To make up: trim across the
corners and fold the excess
canvas over to the wrong side.

2 Cut the felt to size and sew in
place using buttonhole stitch.
Bring the ends together and
buttonhole stitch through the
previous stitching to complete.

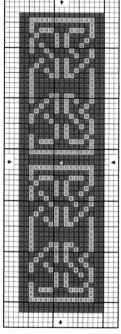

Anchor	
⊞⊞	276
▦	70
☆	Middle point

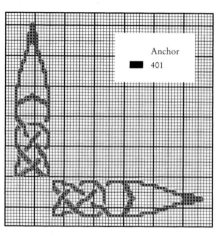

Anchor	
■	401

NAPKIN

This Celtic knot design is quick and easy to sew.
Finish the napkins with a simple frayed edge.

WORKING THE CROSS STITCH

Tack (baste) guidelines 5 cm (2 in) in from the edge along two sides of the linen. Work the design in the corner as shown using two strands of cotton over two threads. Press gently on the reverse side when complete.

1 To make up: cut along the grain about 4 cm (1½ in) from the stitching to give a straight edge to the napkin. Withdraw the linen threads to make a 2½ cm (1 in) deep fringe all round.

YOU WILL NEED

40 cm (16 in) square of pale grey 28 count evenweave linen

tacking (basting) thread

needle

tapestry needle

stranded cotton Anchor 401

small embroidery hoop (flexihoop)

scissors

CHAIR COVER

Renovate a worn mahogany chair cover with this warm and comfortable wool cross stitch design. This cover fits a standard-sized dining room chair with a drop-in seat.

YOU WILL NEED

56 cm (22 in) square of 7 count Sudan canvas

tacking (basting) thread

rotating frame

tapestry needle

tapestry wool DMC 5 skeins of 7406, 4 skeins of 7472, 4 skeins of 7544, 7 skeins of 7590, 9 skeins of 7591

scissors

upholsterer's tacks

hammer

56 cm (22 in) square of calico

padded seat frame

WORKING THE CROSS STITCH

Tack (baste) guidelines across the centre of the canvas in both directions. Fit the canvas onto a rotating frame and work the cross stitch, beginning in the centre. Once the cross stitch is complete, block the embroidered panel to even out the stitches and square up the canvas. Press on the reverse side.

1 To make up: beginning in the middle of the front edge, stretch the canvas over the padded seat frame and secure on the underside with a tack. Working out from the centre, hammer tacks in every 5 cm (2 ins). Repeat the process on the rear of the seat and then stretch the sides. Trim away any excess canvas on the corners to reduce the bulk.

2 Tack a square of calico to the underside to finish.

	DMC		DMC
77	7472	11	7590
--	7406	22	7544
■■	7591	☆	Middle point

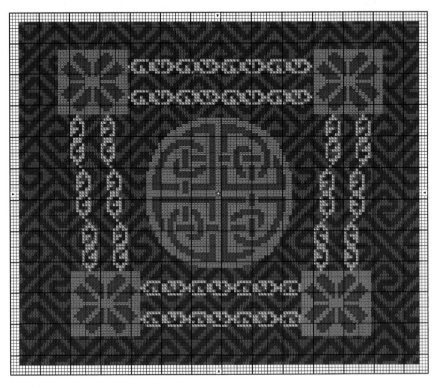

LADY IN THE TOWER

This simple, elegant design was inspired by the rich colours
of a medieval illuminated manuscript.

YOU WILL NEED

25 x 30 cm (10 x 12 in) white
22 count Hardanger

tacking (basting) thread

needle

scissors

stranded cotton DMC 310,
317, 321, 353, 415, 434,
740, 743, 798, 912

tapestry needle

interlocking bar frame

mount board (backing board)

craft knife

strong thread

picture frame

WORKING THE CROSS STITCH

Tack (baste) guidelines across the centre of the
Hardanger in both directions. Beginning in the
centre, work the cross stitches over two pairs of
threads using three strands of cotton.

1 To make up: once
the cross stitch is
complete, work the back
stitch using three strands
of cotton.

2 Remove the tacking
(basting) thread.
Press on the wrong side.
Cut the mount board
(backing board) to the
required size. Stretch
the embroidery and fit it
into a frame which
complements the design.

	DMC		DMC		Backstitch
⹀⹀	353	⹀⹀	798	—	310
⠿	321	╱╱	310		
▷◁	740	╲╲	415	☆	Middle
◯◯	743	⼌⼌	317		point
⬚⬚	912	∧∧	434		

ILLUMINATED LETTER

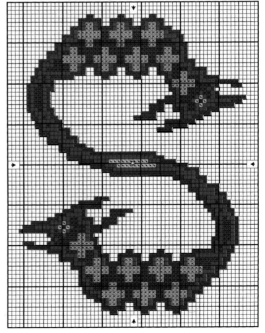

Complete this project with a simple pine frame, painted to match one of the embroidery thread colours.

YOU WILL NEED

15 cm (6 in) square of cream 28 count evenweave linen

tacking (basting) thread

needle

stranded cotton DMC 312, 367, 3046, 3721

tapestry needle

gold thread DMC Art.284

pine frame

paint, e.g. Colourman 102

paint brush

mount board (backing board)

craft knife

strong thread

WORKING THE CROSS STITCH

Tack (baste) guidelines across the centre of the linen in both directions. Work the cross stitch design over one thread using single strands of cotton and double strands of gold thread.

1 To make up: remove the tacking (basting) thread and press lightly on the wrong side.

2 Paint the frame with two coats of paint to match the embroidery and allow to dry.

3 Cut the mount board (backing board) to size. Lay the mount board on the reverse side of the linen, checking that the design is in the centre. Stretch the embroidery and fit into the frame.

	DMC		DMC
	3721		367
	3046		312
	Art.284	☆	Middle point

CELTIC BAG

*This versatile bag looks attractive, but it is also
very practical, and strong enough to carry the vegetables and even a bag
of potatoes home.*

YOU WILL NEED

scissors

*50 cm (¹/₂ yd) Antique Aida
27 count Linda, Zweigart
E1235*

tacking (basting) thread

needle

*stranded cotton DMC 335,
400, 772, 783, 800, 890, 931,
938, 988, 3750*

tapestry needle

embroidery hoop (frame)

*18 cm (7 in) square of
lightweight iron-on interfacing*

sewing thread

150 cm (¹/₂ yd) calico lining

sewing machine

WORKING THE CROSS STITCH

Cut two 41 x 45 cm (16 x 18 in) pieces of linen for the bag. Tack (baste) a guideline lengthways down the centre of one piece. Mark the top edge of the bag by tacking a line crossways 4¹/₂ cm (1³/₄ in) down from the top. Tack a guideline crossways in the centre of the marked panel. Beginning in the centre, work the cross stitches over two threads using two strands of thread. The backstitches are worked in several different colours – body 938, tail 3750 and tongue 355. When the embroidery is complete, press on the wrong side. Ensure the design is square on before ironing the interfacing onto the reverse side. This will help to stabilize the embroidery.

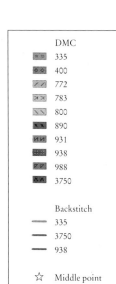

DMC	
= =	335
◊ ◊	400
⁄ ⁄	772
⋉ ⋊	783
＼ ＼	800
⬎ ⬑	890
И И	931
▦ ▦	938
⁊ ⁊	988
◮ ◭	3750

Backstitch
—— 335
—— 3750
—— 938

☆ Middle point

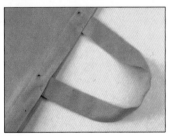

1 To make up: with right sides together, sew down both sides and across the bottom. Trim across the corners and press the seams flat. Make a lining in the same way using two 41 cm (16 in) squares of calico, then stitch again just outside the first row of stitches for extra strength.

2 Fold over 12 mm (½ in) at the top edge of the bag, fold over again along the tacked line and press. Turn the bag through to the right side and insert the calico lining, tucking it under the folded edge. Pin, tack and top stitch along both edges of the hem.

3 Cut two 10 x 45 cm (4 x 18 in) pieces of linen for the straps. Fold them in half lengthways and stitch 12 mm (½ in) from the cut edge, leaving the ends open. Press the seam open and turn through. Press again making sure that that the seam lies down the centre. Zig-zag across the ends. Pin the handles 10 cm (4 in) in from each edge and stitch securely.

COVERED BUTTONS

Add a touch of elegance to a plain black coat or cardigan
with these sparkly medieval buttons. This design will cover 3 cm
(1¼ in) buttons, but could be adapted for other sizes.

YOU WILL NEED

black 27 count Linda,
Zweigart E1235

tapestry needle

stranded cotton Anchor white

fine antique gold braid
Kreinik 221

small embroidery hoop
(flexihoop)

scissors

thin card (cardboard)

quilter's pencil

needle

sewing thread

3 cm (1¼ in)
self-cover buttons

WORKING THE CROSS STITCH

Work each button design within a 5 cm (2 in) area
and press on the reverse side when completed.

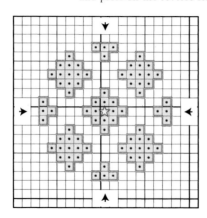

Anchor

• • White

Backstitch

— Kreinik Antique
Gold 221 fine braid

☆ Middle point

1 To make up: cut out a 4 cm (1½ in)
card (cardboard) circle and then cut
out a smaller circle in the centre to make
a card ring. (This lets you see the centre
of the stitches). Position the card ring over
the embroidery and draw round the
outside of it with a pencil.

2 Cut out the button cover and work a
row of tiny running stitches round
the edge. Lay the button on the reverse
side of the cover, pull up the stitches
tightly and secure. Press the back onto the
button to complete.

STOOL COVER

*Add a soft, warm cover to a simple wooden stool or use
the finished design to upholster a footstool.*

YOU WILL NEED

*40 cm (16 in) square of
7 count Sudan canvas*

rotating frame

tacking (basting) thread

needle

scissors

tapestry needle

*tapestry wool Anchor 6 skeins of
8024, 2 skeins each of 8016,
8106 and 8138, 1 skein of 8136*

*28 cm (11 in) square of thick
wadding (batting)*

double-sided tape

28 cm (11 in) diameter stool

*1 m (1 yd) of 3 cm (1¼ in)
wide dark brown braid*

sewing thread

WORKING THE CROSS STITCH

Tack (baste) guidelines across the
centre of the canvas in both directions
and work the cross stitch in wool.

Once the cross stitch is complete,
block the design to even out the
stitches and trim to 4 cm (1½ in).

1 To make up: cut the
wadding (batting) to
fit the top of the stool. Put
double-sided tape round
the side rim of the stool.
Stretch the cover over the
wadding and stick down,
keeping the stitching just
over the edge.

2 Stitch the braid
invisibly along the
top edge and then sew the
ends securely.

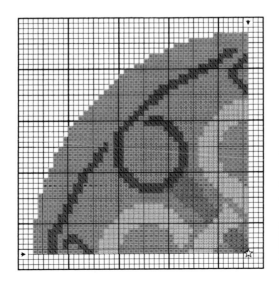

Anchor	
⹀ ⹀	8024
◇ ◇	8136
◥ ◥	8106
⊡ ⊡	8016
▶ ▶	8138
☆	Middle point

ALPHABET BLOCK

Babies and toddlers will love this big, chunky brick.
It's easy to catch and so soft it won't hurt anyone.

YOU WILL NEED

18 x 109 cm (7 x 43 in) navy
14 count Aida, Zweigart E3246

scissors

tacking (basting) thread

needle

embroidery hoop (frame)

coton perlé no.5 DMC 554,
718, 725, 995, 996

stranded cotton DMC 823

tapestry needle

spray starch

sewing thread

polyester stuffing

WORKING THE CROSS STITCH

Cut the Aida into 18 cm (7 in) squares and bind the edges to prevent fraying. Tack (baste) guidelines in the centre of each panel and work the cross stitch in coton perlé. Once complete, work the backstitch with two strands of stranded cotton. Press and spray starch onto the reverse side.

DMC	
▤▤	554
▦▦	996
▶◀	725
◉◉	718
◣◥	995
Backstitch	
——	823
☆	Middle point

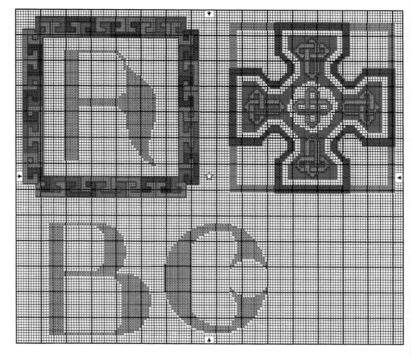

1 To make up: trim round each panel leaving four squares of Aida showing. Stitch the squares together as illustrated in the template section and turn the cube through to the right side. Ease out the corners and fill with stuffing.

2 Slip stitch the last two edges together and pat into shape.

GIFT TAG

*Using the waste canvas technique, this handsome medieval bird
could also be used to decorate a man's tie.*

YOU WILL NEED

*15 cm (6 in) square of grey/blue
28 count Jobelan*

needle

*stranded cotton DMC 739,
740, 817, 3808*

tapestry needle

scissors

*small embroidery hoop
(flexihoop)*

tacking (basting) thread

stiff card (cardboard)

all-purpose glue

red gift tag

	DMC
⬒⬒	739
▷▷	740
▭▭	3808
◐◐	817
	French knot
◉	739
☆	Middle point

WORKING THE CROSS STITCH

Mark guidelines across the centre of the
linen in both directions. Work the cross
stitch over two threads using two strands of
cotton. Once the cross stitch is complete,
press on the wrong side before working the
French knots.

1 To make up: measure the embroidered
panel and cut a piece of stiff card
(cardboard) the same size. Trim the fabric round
the embroidery to 2 cm (¾ in) and stretch over
the card, mitring the corners carefully. Stick the
covered card onto the gift tag.

BOOKMARK

Any book-lover would be delighted to receive this beautiful, tasselled medieval bookmark which will bring a distinguished academic air to any paperback.

WORKING THE CROSS STITCH

Mark the centre of the stitching paper with a soft pencil and work the cross stitch design using three strands of cotton.

NEEDLEWORK TIP

Be careful when using stitching paper since it tends to rip easily if you have to unpick stitches. The paper can be repaired if necessary with sticky tape and the holes repunched using a sharp needle.

YOU WILL NEED

8 x 20 cm (3 x 8 in) stitching
paper

soft pencil

tapestry needle

stranded cotton DMC 311, 312,
367, 918, 3046, 3722

scissors

5 cm (2 in) square of card
(cardboard)

1 To make up: once the design has been completed trim away the excess paper. Any paper remaining visible can be coloured using a felt pen.

2 Cut a 50 cm (20 in) length of each embroidery thread colour and separate out the strands. Wind the threads round the card (cardboard) and make a tassel to sew onto one end of the bookmark to complete.

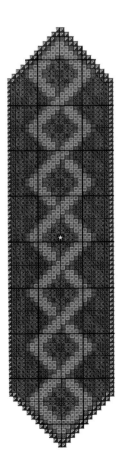

	DMC
◣◥	918
◪◩	311
◉◉	312
◥◤	3722
▦▦	367
══	3046
☆	Middle point

SEWING KIT

Be prepared for any small repair jobs with this handy sewing kit which keeps everything you need together in one place.

YOU WILL NEED

18 x 38 cm (7 x 15 in) black 14 count Aida

embroidery hoop (frame)

tapestry needle

sewing thread

stranded cotton DMC 3 skeins 972, 1 skein each of 321, 796, 909, 995

scissors

28 x 69 cm (11 x 27 in) black iron-on interfacing

40 cm (16 in) square of black felt

5 x 13 cm (2 x 5 in) piece of wadding (batting)

5 x 13 cm (2 x 5 in) piece of stiff card (cardboard)

all-purpose glue

2 m (2¼ yd) of 25 mm (1 in) wide black bias binding

sewing machine

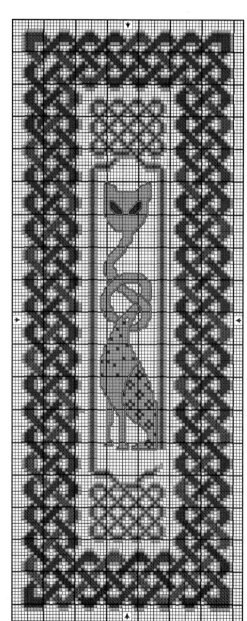

WORKING THE CROSS STITCH

Mark guidelines across the centre of the Aida in both directions and work the cross stitch using two strands of cotton. Work the backstitch with two strands of turquoise (995). Press on the reverse side.

DMC	
▤▤	321
▸◂	995
◤◥	796
⋮⋮⋮	972
◡◡	909

Backstitch	
—	995

☆ Middle point

1 To make up: cut a piece of interfacing the same size as the Aida and iron onto the wrong side. Cut one piece of felt the same size, one 10 x 30 cm (4 x 12 in), another 10 x 18 cm (4 x 7 in) and the last piece 10 x 13 cm (4 x 5 in). Stick the wadding (batting) to the card (cardboard) and lay on top of the small piece of felt. Trim across the corners, stretch the felt and stick the flaps down.

2 Iron interfacing onto one side of the 10 x 30 cm (4 x 12 in) piece of felt for added strength and stitch in place on the backing felt. Pin the needle flap in position, lay the pin cushion pad along one edge and stitch securely.

3 Tack (baste) the completed felt backing onto the wrong side of the Aida. Stitch 3 mm (¼ in) all round, then remove the tacking (basting) thread. Fold a 76 cm (30 in) length of bias binding in half lengthways. Tuck in the ends and stitch close to the edge to make the ties. Fold the binding in half and tack in the middle of one end of the Aida. Pin and tack the rest of the bias binding round the edge of the sewing kit, mitring the corners neatly. Machine close to the edge of the binding to complete.

CELTIC KNOT
SAMPLER

This unusual design features nine different Celtic knots.
You could stitch them individually to make a set of greetings cards.

YOU WILL NEED

*25 cm (10 in) square of beige
28 count evenweave linen*

tacking (basting) thread

needle

*stranded cotton Anchor 187,
229*

tapestry needle

embroidery hoop (frame)

*20 cm (8 in) square of mount
board (backing board)*

strong thread

picture frame

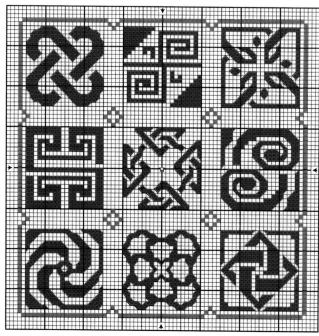

WORKING THE CROSS STITCH

Tack (baste) guidelines across the
centre of the linen in both directions
and work the cross stitch over two
threads using two strands of cotton.
Press the embroidery on the reverse
side when complete.

1 To make up: stretch the piece of
embroidery over the mount board
(backing board).

2 Fit the sampler into a frame
which complements the design.

Anchor		
▬ 229	☆	Middle point
▦ 187		

CELTIC CROSS

The Highlands of Scotland, with their wild landscapes and beautiful sunsets, are the backdrop for this quintessential Celtic cross.

	Anchor
▬▬	393
▦▦	905
▷▷	129
◦◦	279
◥◥	923
▽▽	48
╱╱	342
▬▬	862
☆	Middle point

YOU WILL NEED

25 x 30 cm (10 x 12 in) pale blue 14 count Aida

tacking (basting) thread

needle

stranded cotton Anchor 48, 129, 279, 342, 393, 862, 923, 905

tapestry needle

embroidery hoop (frame)

18 x 23 cm (7 x 9 in) mount board (backing board)

strong thread

picture frame

WORKING THE CROSS STITCH

Tack (baste) guidelines across the centre of the Aida in both directions and work the cross stitch using two strands of cotton. Press the embroidery on the wrong side.

1 To make up: stretch the embroidery over the mount board (backing board).

2 Fit the design into a frame which complements it to complete.

BYZANTINE GIFT BAG

This little bag is the ideal size to hold a brooch or earrings.
The design was adapted from a Byzantine Gospel book.

YOU WILL NEED

40 cm (16 in) of 8 cm (3 in)
natural linen band,
Inglestone Collection 983/80

tacking (basting) thread

needle

stranded cotton Anchor 44,
306, 861

sewing thread

tapestry needle

pins

scissors

50 cm (20 in) ochre yellow cord

WORKING THE CROSS STITCH

Tack (baste) a guideline across the linen 15 cm (6 in) from one end and mark the centre line lengthways. This is the front of the bag and the motif faces towards the short end. Work the cross stitch and backstitch over two threads using two strands of thread. Once this is complete, press the embroidery on the wrong side and work the French knots as shown.

Anchor		French knots
	306	knots
	44	306
	861	861
☆	Middle point	

1 To make up: fold over 5 cm (2 in) to the wrong side at both ends. Turn under 1 cm (³⁄₈ in) and pin in place. Stitch across the hem close to the turned edge and again 1 cm (³⁄₈ in) away to make a casing for the cord.

2 Fold the band in half crossways, with right side facing out. Stitch down both sides as far as the casing line.

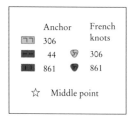

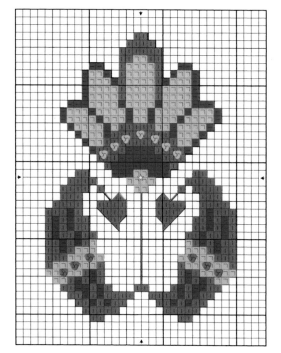

3 Cut the cord in two. Thread one piece through one way and then thread the other in the opposite direction. Tie the ends together with an overhand knot and unravel the ends to form simple tassels.

MEDIEVAL DOG PICTURE

This fascinating seventh century design has a dog whose tongue and tail have been elongated and interlaced to form an intricate pattern.

YOU WILL NEED

25 x 25 cm (10 x 10 in) cream 14 count Aida

stranded cotton Anchor 100, 310, 351, 859, 890

tapestry needle

interlocking bar frame

scissors

18 x 21 cm (7 x 8¼ in) mount board (backing board)

strong thread

picture frame

WORKING THE CROSS STITCH

Tack (baste) guidelines across the centre of the Aida in both directions and work the cross stitch and backstitch using two strands of thread. Press on the wrong side.

1 To make up: stretch the embroidery over the mount board (backing board) and fit in a suitable frame.

	Anchor			Anchor
▦	310		▨	859
▥	351			Backstitch
▶	890		—	351
◪	100			
			☆	Middle point

LABYRINTH
PAPERWEIGHT

*This Celtic labyrinth design was inspired by a 300 BC coin from
Knossos in Crete, home of the mythical Minotaur.*

YOU WILL NEED

*10 cm (4 in) square of 18 count
single canvas*

tacking (basting) thread

needle

coton perlé no.3 DMC 307, 796

tapestry needle

scissors

all-purpose glue

*7 cm (2½ in) clear glass
paperweight*

8 cm (3 in) square of blue felt

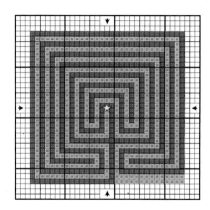

NEEDLEWORK TIP

The perlé thread is
quite thick for this
gauge of canvas, but it
produces an attractive
raised stitch.

WORKING THE CROSS STITCH

Tack (baste) guidelines across the
centre of the canvas in both directions
and work the cross stitch using a single
strand of coton perlé.

1 To make up: trim the canvas to fit
the bottom of the paperweight
and stick in place around the outer edge.
Cut the felt to size and glue over the
canvas to complete.

	DMC
▨▨	307
▧▧	796
☆	Middle point

BLACKWORK FRAME

Display a treasured old photograph in this tiny little frame. For a richer effect, work the embroidery over the whole of the frame area.

YOU WILL NEED

30 x 60 cm (12 x 24 in) cream 27 count Linda, Zweigart E1235

scissors

needle

sewing thread

stranded cotton Anchor 403

fine gold braid Kreinik 002

tapestry needle

20 cm (8 in) square of mount board (backing board)

craft knife

safety ruler

30 x 60 cm (12 x 24 in) calico

WORKING THE CROSS STITCH

Cut a 15 x 30 cm (6 x 12 in) piece of linen. Tack (baste) guidelines across the centre in both directions. Work the cross stitch using two strands of cotton and the backstitch using one strand of black or gold thread. Press on the reverse side.

1 To make up: measure the outside edge of the embroidered panel and cut two pieces of mount board (backing board) that size. Measure the size of the centre panel and the distance from each edge. Use these measurements to cut a window in one piece of card (cardboard).

2 Trim the embroidered panel about 2½ cm (1 in) from the stitching. Cut into the corners of the window and stretch over the mount board frame. Stretch linen over the other piece of mount board.

3 Cut two pieces of calico 12 mm (½ in) larger than the frame and press over the turnings. Pin in place on the back of each part of the frame and hem. Oversew the two sections of the frame together along three sides.

4 Make a stand by scoring a piece of card 2½ cm (1 in) from the end and covering it in calico. Oversew the stand onto the back of the frame to complete.

Anchor		Backstitch
■	403	— Anchor 403
☆	Middle point	— Kreinik 002

EMBROIDERED BLOUSE

These medieval motifs were inspired by the Book of Hours and will match the waistcoat on the following page.

WORKING THE CROSS STITCH

Make the blouse using a similar pattern or adapt a bought one to suit the design. Trim the seam allowance off the cuff and neck facing pattern pieces. Lay the pieces on 14 count graph paper and draw an outline, then transfer any pattern markings. Draw one red flower in the centre of the cuff and space both small flowers on either side. Draw out the motifs for the neck facing on separate graph paper. Cut carefully round the motifs and arrange them on the pattern outline, keeping them at least two squares from the edge, and stick them in place.

YOU WILL NEED

white medieval-style blouse

scissors

14 count graph paper

pencil

double-sided tape

needle

tacking (basting) thread

tapestry needle

sewing thread

*stranded cotton Anchor white,
133, 246, 290, 335, 369, 380,
397, 398, 400, 403*

embroidery hoop (frame)

*30 cm (¹/₃ yd) black 27 count
Linda, Zweigart E1235*

pins

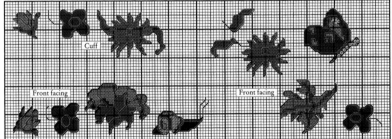

Anchor	
■	403
▦	400
▤	398
◇◇	397
••	white
▽▽	290
◢◢	246
■	133
▥	380
∧∧	369
✕✕	335

Backstitch	
—	403
—	246

1 Draw an outline of the pattern pieces on the linen and tack (baste) a central guideline. Work the cross stitch and the backstitch using two strands of cotton over two threads of linen.

2 To make up: once complete, press on the wrong side and cut out adding 1¹/₂ cm (⁵/₈ in) seam allowances all round. Turn under the seam allowance, snipping the curves and tack close to the edge.

3 Pin and tack onto the blouse and slip stitch in place. Make a small loop from a bias strip to fasten the cuffs and neck opening and sew on the buttons to complete the fastenings.

WAISTCOAT

*This stunning design could also be added to an existing waistcoat
using the waste canvas technique.*

YOU WILL NEED

*75 cm (⅞ yd) black 27 count
Linda, Zweigart E1235*

75 cm (⅞ yd) lining fabric

scissors

needle

sewing thread

sewing machine

14 count graph paper

pencil

double-sided tape

pins

tacking (basting) thread

*stranded cotton Anchor 3 skeins
each of white and 397, 2 skeins
of 398 and one each of 133,
246, 290, 335, 369, 380,
400, 403*

WORKING THE CROSS STITCH

Enlarge the pattern pieces or use
a simple bought pattern and cut
out the waistcoat front in linen.
Sew the darts and press towards
the centre. Trim the seam
allowance from the pattern piece,
then draw an outline on 14 count
graph paper and transfer any
pattern markings. Draw out the
motifs on separate graph paper.
Cut carefully round them and
arrange on the pattern outline
keeping them at least two squares
from the edge. Once you are
satisfied with the arrangement,
stick them in place. Mark the
outline of the unicorn and work
the cross stitch from the chart.
Sew the backstitch to finish the
embroidery. Work the other side
of the waistcoat as a mirror image
of the first side and press both
front panels on the reverse side.

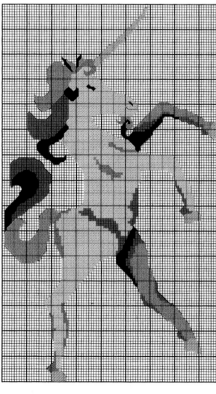

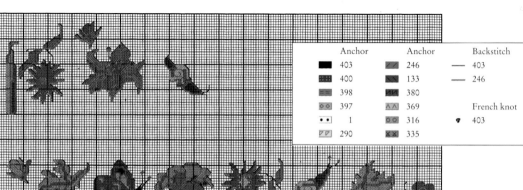

Anchor		Anchor		Backstitch	
■	403	⁄⁄	246	—	403
▦	400	◤◥	133	—	246
⩵	398	⩘⩘	380		
◌◌	397	⋀⋀	369		French knot
••	1	◦◦	316	♥	403
⫽⫽	290	⤬⤬	335		

1 To make up: cut out the front lining and two backs in lining fabric. Sew all the darts and press. With right sides together, stitch the front lining to the linen leaving the shoulder and side seams free. Stitch the back pieces together along the armhole edge, the neck edge and the bottom. Trim the seam allowances and snip across the corners before turning through.

Pin and sew the back and front together at the shoulder and side seams, leaving the lining free. Trim the seams and press flat.

2 Turn under the lining seam allowance and slip stitch. Press the waistcoat on the reverse side and add a fastening if required.

CELTIC
AND
MEDIEVAL

MONASTIC
BELL PULL

*The beads on this beautiful design catch the light
and give it a special richness.*

YOU WILL NEED

*25 x 92 cm (10 x 36 in) navy
14 count Aida, Zweigart E3706*

rotating frame

needle

tacking (basting) thread

scissors

tapestry needle

*Anchor Marlitt 3 skeins of 817,
1007 and 5 skeins of 859*

*two packets of glass seed beads,
Mill Hill shade 02009*

*fine metallic braid Kreinik 012,
026*

*silver thread Madeira no.5 9805
shade 10*

sewing thread

sewing machine

tailor's chalk

*two packets of frosted glass
beads, Mill Hill shade 62034*

pins

*25 x 92 cm (10 x 36 in)
navy cotton backing fabric*

*8½ x 13½ cm (3¼ x 5¼ in)
card (cardboard)*

30 cm (12 in) silver cord

WORKING THE CROSS STITCH

Tack (baste) a guideline lengthways
down the centre of the Aida. Begin
stitching about 13 cm (5 in) from the
top using two strands of Marlitt. Work
all the cross stitch and then the

Smyrna cross stitch. Once these are
complete, sew on the beads and finally
work the backstitch. Remove the
embroidery from the rotating frame
and block if necessary.

	Anchor Marlitt
	1007
	817
	859
	Madiera metallic silver
—	9805
	Kreinik metallic
	balger fine braid 026
	balger fine braid 012
	Mill Hill beads
	62034
	02009

Centre repeat

70

1 To make up: tack a guideline down both sides of the embroidery about 1½ cm (½ in) from the stitching. Mark the point of the bell pull 3½ cm (1½ in) down from the stitching and draw a diagonal line from this mark to the side guidelines. Complete the tacking (basting) and pin to the cotton backing with the right sides together. Stitch round the bell pull along the guideline leaving it open at the top. Trim the seams and cut across the corners before turning through.

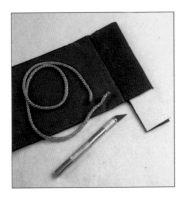

2 Ease out the corners and press on the reverse side. Turn over a 6 cm (2½ in) hem and stitch securely by hand. Score the card (cardboard) in the middle lengthways and insert into the hem. Thread the cord through, tie the ends together and tuck inside the hem. Make a tassel and stitch it to the point of the bell pull to finish off.

TRINKET BOWL

This pretty frosted glass bowl is decorated with a Celtic motif adapted from a design on an ornate Saxon dagger.

YOU WILL NEED

15 cm (6 in) square of antique white 28 count Cashel linen, Zweigart E3281

tacking (basting) thread

needle

tapestry needle

small embroidery frame (flexihoop)

stranded cotton DMC 926, 3808

fine antique gold braid Kreinik 221

9 cm (3½ in) frosted glass bowl, Framecraft GT4

	Kreinik fine braid
🔲	Antique gold 221
	DMC
▬	3808
◼◼	926
	French knot
●	926
☆	Middle point

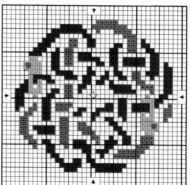

WORKING THE CROSS STITCH

Tack (baste) guidelines across the centre of the linen in both directions. Work the cross stitch using two strands of cotton and a single strand of gold thread. Press on the reverse side and then work the French knots to complete the design.

1 To make up: fit the piece of embroidery into the lid of the glass bowl following the manufacturer's instructions.

GREETINGS CARD

The Book of Kells is a rich source of inspiration for medieval embroidery and these two loving doves are just one example.

YOU WILL NEED

15 cm (6 in) square of cream 28 count evenweave linen

tacking (basting) thread

needle

small embroidery hoop (flexihoop)

tapestry needle

stranded cotton DMC 367, 3046, 3722

scissors

7 cm (2¾ in) square of cream felt

greetings card with a 6½ cm (2½ in) opening

double-sided tape

❖ ❖ ❖ ❖ ❖

NEEDLECRAFT TIP

Use double-sided tape to mount the embroidered panel to prevent the card from buckling.

WORKING THE CROSS STITCH

Tack (baste) guidelines across the centre in both directions. Work the cross stitch using one strand of cotton over single threads of linen.

1 To make up: press on the reverse side once complete and trim to fit inside the card. Trim the felt to the size of the opening and stick on the inside flap. Use double-sided tape to stick the embroidery behind the opening and stick the flap down firmly.

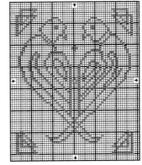

DMC	
▨	3722
▨	3046
▨	367
☆	Middle point

MEDIEVAL CLOCK

*This clock design was inspired by the magnificent architecture and
bright colourful stained glass windows found in medieval churches.*

YOU WILL NEED

*25 x 30 cm (10 x 12 in) black
14 count Aida*

tacking (basting) thread

needle

tapestry needle

interlocking bar frame

*2 reels of fine Aztec gold braid
Kreinik 202HL*

*stranded cotton DMC 340,
347, 351, 444, 445, 988, 995,
996, 3348, 3746*

*25 x 30 cm (10 x 12 in)
lightweight iron-on interfacing*

*MDF (medium density
fibreboard) clock base and
mechanism, Decorative Arts
W122*

blackboard paint

paintbrush

scissors

pins

tailor's chalk

all-purpose glue

WORKING THE CROSS STITCH

Tack (baste) guidelines across the
centre of the Aida in both directions.
Work the cross stitch using two strands
of cotton and one strand of gold braid.
The central stitch on the chart is
shown for reference only to ensure
accurate placement of the clock
mechanism at the end of the project.
Once complete, press on the reverse
side and iron on the interfacing.

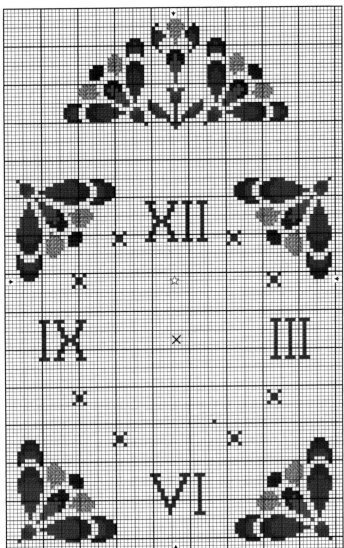

1 To make up: paint the MDF clock base with two coats of blackboard paint and leave to dry.

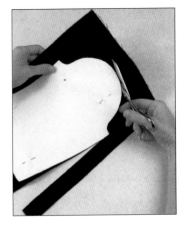

2 Make a pattern by pressing a piece of A4 paper over the clock base. Cut around the marked line and cut out the centre hole. Lay the pattern on the embroidery. Once you have checked it is central and square, pin in place and cut out carefully.

3 Spread glue over the MDF base and stick down the embroidered panel. Make a cord using a reel of fine braid. Stick this round the rim, trim the ends and tuck underneath the Aida. Snip away the fabric covering the hole and fit the clock mechanism following the manufacturer's instructions.

DMC		
340		996
347		3348
351		3746
444		Kreinik fine
445		braid 202HL
988		
995	☆	Middle point

WOOL SCARF

*This motif comes from the border design of a splendid
illuminated manuscript from the renowned Winchester school
of the early eleventh century.*

YOU WILL NEED

dark green wool scarf

*10 cm (4 in) square
of 14 count waste canvas*

tacking (basting) thread

scissors

embroidery needle

*stranded cotton Anchor 891,
901*

fine gold braid Kreinik 002

sewing thread

*10 cm (4 in) square of
dark green felt*

	Anchor
4 4	901
▽ ▽	891
—	Kreinik fine gold braid 002
☆	Middle point

WORKING THE CROSS STITCH

Tack (baste) the waste canvas centrally at one end of
the scarf about 5 cm (2 in) up from the fringe. Work
the cross stitch using two strands of cotton. Take
care to sew the stitches as evenly as possible, bringing
the needle up exactly where the last stitch finished.

1 To make up: once
complete, remove the
waste canvas thread by
thread. This will be easier
if you manipulate the
canvas first to loosen the
threads. Work the
backstitch using a single
strand of gold braid.

2 Press the embroidery
on the reverse side
once complete. Cut a
circle from the dark green
felt to cover the back of
the embroidery and then
sew invisibly to the scarf.

Spiral tray cloth

This early medieval design is typical of those from Iona, Scotland, and illustrated in The Book of Durrow.

YOU WILL NEED

*25 x 40 cm (10 x 16 in) sage
27 count evenweave linen*

tacking (basting) thread

needle

tapestry needle

embroidery hoop (frame)

*stranded cotton Anchor 118,
300, 307, 969*

scissors

sewing thread

WORKING
THE CROSS STITCH

Tack (baste) guidelines across the centre of the linen in both directions. Work the cross stitch and backstitch using two strands of cotton over two threads.

1 To make up: when complete, press the embroidery on the wrong side. Turn under a 12 mm (½ in) hem on all edges, mitring the corners and stitch in place by hand or sewing machine.

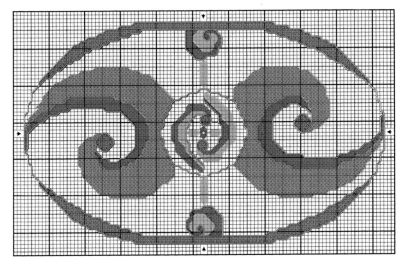

Anchor	
☰	118
⣿	300
✕	307
◎	969

Backstitch	
—	307

☆ Middle point

SPECTACLE CASE

Your spectacles will never be lost again
if kept in this attractive case which can be hung around your neck.

YOU WILL NEED

23 x 28 cm (9 x 11 in)
12 count single thread canvas

tacking (basting) thread

needle

coton perlé no.5 DMC 3 skeins
of 930, 1 skein each of 310, 321
783, 796, 972

coton à broder DMC 745

gold thread DMC Art.284

tapestry needle

scissors

sewing thread

needle

23 x 28 cm (9 x 11 in) heavy
duty iron-on interfacing

23 x 28 cm (9 x 11 in) tie silk or
similar fabric

1 m (1 yd) 5 mm (¼ in) cord

WORKING THE CROSS STITCH

Tack (baste) guidelines across the centre of the canvas in both directions. Work the perlé cross stitch on the birds first, then use the coton à broder to fill in. Finally work the background. Press the embroidery on the wrong side and trim the canvas to 1 cm (½ in). Snip into curves, turn the edges in and tack.

1 To make up: cut two pieces of interfacing 8.3 x 17.2 cm (3¼ x 6¾ in) and round off the corners. Iron these onto the silk and cut out leaving a 1 cm (½ in) seam allowance. Turn the edges over and tack carefully, easing in the fullness at the corners.

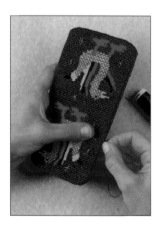

2 Put the canvas and lining pieces together with right sides facing out and oversew the edges. Once both are stitched round, put the spectacle case together and oversew with coton perlé 930, starting and finishing 5 cm (2 in) down from the top edge.

	DMC
▨▨	310
1 1	783
4 4	972
▶◀	796
◥◣	930
○○	321
⊠⊠	coton à broder 745

Backstitch
— DMC Art.284

☆ Middle point

3 Tie a knot in the cord 4 cm (1½ in) from the end and tease out the end. Take the frayed ends over the knot and tie tightly, then pull the ends back down over the knot and wrap thread round them to make a waist for the tassel. Repeat at the other end, trim the ends neatly and stitch to each side of the spectacle case as shown.

RINGBEARER'S CUSHION

This delightful Celtic design could be stitched in two complementary colours to match the bridesmaids' dresses or the wedding flowers.

YOU WILL NEED

30 cm (12 in) square of antique white 28 count linen

tacking (basting) thread

needle

stranded cotton DMC 224, 3685

tapestry needle

embroidery hoop (frame)

1 m (1¼ yd) of 2 cm (¾ in) wine coloured ribbon

1 m (1¼ yd) piping cord

sewing thread

sewing machine

scissors

30 cm (12 in) square of antique white backing fabric

polyester stuffing

1 m (1¼ yd) 3 mm (¼ in) wine coloured ribbon

WORKING THE CROSS STITCH

Tack (baste) guidelines across the centre of the linen in both directions. Work the centre motif using two strands of cotton. Count out the threads carefully and stitch the border. Press on the reverse side.

1 To make up: fold the wide ribbon over the piping cord and tack in position round the edge of the cushion 2 cm (¾ in) away from the cross stitch. Stitch the piping in place along one side. With right sides facing, sew the cushion cover together along the remaining three sides. Trim across the corners and turn through. Give the cushion a final press and fill with stuffing.

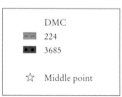

2 Slip stitch the opening. Cut the narrow ribbon in half, find the middle of each half and sew securely in the centre of the cross. Stitch a decorative cross stitch on top to finish.

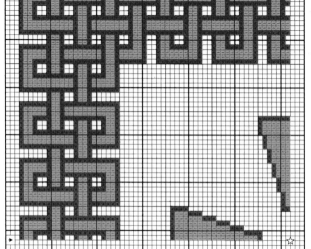

DMC	
– –	224
●●	3685
☆	Middle point

CHESSBOARD

The black squares are stitched in Assisi embroidery,
a variation of cross stitch where the design areas are left blank and the
background is filled with cross stitch.

YOU WILL NEED

38 cm (15 in) square of white
14 count Aida

tacking (basting) thread

needle

scissors

embroidery hoop (frame)

stranded cotton Anchor 403

tapestry needle

safety ruler

30 x 60 cm (12 x 24 in)
mount board (backing board)

craft knife

strong thread

all-purpose glue

125 cm (1 1/3 yd) black cord

WORKING THE CROSS STITCH

Tack (baste) guidelines across the centre of the Aida in
both directions and work the cross stitch using two
strands of cotton. Press the embroidery on the wrong side.

1 To make up: measure
the length of two
adjacent sides of the embroidery. Cut two pieces of
mount board (backing board)
that size and stretch the
embroidery over one of them.

2 Oversew the cord to
the edge of the chess-
board. Unravel the ends
and stitch them flat underneath the board. Stick the
second piece of mount board
(backing board) to the
bottom of the chessboard to
cover the raw edges.

Anchor
■● ■ 403

BEDSIDE TABLECLOTH

This unusual Celtic design could be repeated on the border of a much larger tablecloth.

YOU WILL NEED

51 cm (20 in) square of cream
28 count evenweave linen

tacking (basting) thread

needle

tapestry needle

scissors

embroidery hoop (frame)

Anchor Marlitt 831, 1140

gold thread DMC Art.284

sewing thread

	Anchor Marlitt
▦	831
▬	1140
	Backstitch
—	DMC Art.284
☆	Middle point

WORKING THE CROSS STITCH

Tack (baste) guidelines across the centre of the linen in both directions. Count the threads out to the border on all four guidelines and double-check the spacing before beginning to sew.

1 To make up: first, sew the cross stitch onto the centre motif using a single strand of Marlitt thread over two threads of linen, then work the backstitch in gold thread. Once the design is complete, press the embroidery on the wrong side.

2 Trim away the excess fabric, leaving 2½ cm (1 in) all round for the hem i.e. a 46 cm (18 in) square. Mitre the corners and make a 12 mm (½ in) hem all round. Tack in position, then hem. Slip stitch the mitred corners and press on the wrong side to finish.

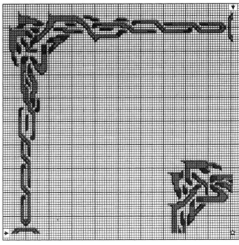

PURSE

This handy little purse with a bold dragon design could be used for
holding game counters, money or a spare lipstick.

YOU WILL NEED

18 x 36 cm (7 x 14 in) black
14 count Aida

scissors

tacking (basting) thread

needle

interlocking bar frame

tapestry needle

stranded cotton DMC white,
742, 744, 900, 910

fine Aztec gold braid
Kreinik 202HL

18 x 36 cm (7 x 14 in) mediun
weight iron-on interfacing

18 x 36 cm (7 x 14 in) black
lining

sewing thread

sewing machine

8 cm (3 in) black zip

WORKING THE CROSS STITCH

Cut an 18 cm (7 in) square of Aida and tack (baste) guidelines across the centre in both directions. Work the cross stitch using two strands of cotton and finish with the backstitch. Once complete, press the reverse side of the embroidery and iron the interfacing onto both pieces of Aida.

1 To make up: draw out a template and use it to cut out two purse shapes from the lining and the Aida, making sure that the cross stitch is positioned within the stitching line.
With right sides together, sew the lining to the Aida along the straight edge. Trim the seams and press open. Pin the two sections together, matching the seams, and stitch round, leaving a 5 cm (2 in) gap in the lining.

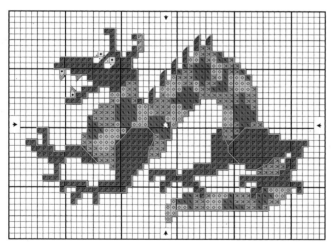

DMC		Backstitch	
•• 1	⊠⊠ 900	—	Kreinik fine
⊠⊠ 742	⊠⊠ 910		braid 202HL
⊙⊙ 744		☆	Middle point

2 Trim the seam allowance and snip the curves before turning through. Slipstitch the lining and tuck it inside the purse. Sew the zip in the opening by hand, using a double length of thread.

BOOK COVER

Inspired by a medieval stone carving this bird design could
be used to cover a small notebook or sketchbook.

YOU WILL NEED

25 x 38 cm (10 x 15 in) cream
14 count Aida

tacking (basting) thread

needle

embroidery hoop (frame)

tapestry needle

stranded cotton Anchor 371,
942, 943

scissors

25 x 38 cm (10 x 15 in) medium
weight iron-on interfacing

small notebook, approximate
size 11 x 15½ cm (4⅜ x 6 in)

pins

double-sided tape

WORKING THE CROSS STITCH

Tack (baste) a guideline crossways
down the middle of the Aida to mark
the position of the book spine. Tack
another line 6 cm (2⅜ in) away
marking the centre of the design. Find
the mid-point of this line and mark

with tacking (basting) thread. Begin
the cross stitch, making sure that the
bird is upright on the right hand side
of the Aida. Once the embroidery is
complete, remove the tacking (basting)
thread and press.

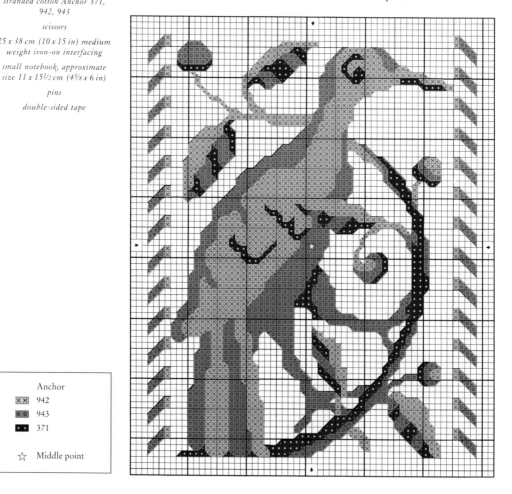

	Anchor
✕✕	942
○○	943
■■	371
☆	Middle point

1 To make up: iron the
interfacing on the reverse side
and mark the position of the book
spine with pins.

2 Lay the fabric face down and
hold the book in line with the
pins. Open the front flap of the book
and trim the fabric to 2½ cm (1 in)
all round. Cut across the corners
1 cm (3/8 in) from the book and snip
into the spine.

3 Stick double-sided tape round
the inside of the cover. First
fold over the corners, then stretch the
cover onto the tape. Repeat on the
other side, making sure that the book
can close easily. Tuck the spare Aida
down inside the spine with the point
of small scissors. Use more double-
sided tape to stick the fly leaf down
on both sides.

BLACKWORK DECORATIONS

Although traditionally black on white or cream fabric, these "Blackwork" Christmas decorations look equally good worked in red on black fabric.

WORKING THE CROSS STITCH

Trace the template and cut out three card (cardboard) shapes for each decoration. Place the shape on the linen and draw three outlines using the vanishing marker pen. Stitch the blackwork design inside the lines and press on the wrong side.

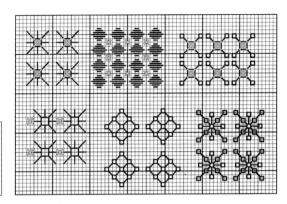

	Anchor		Backstitch		Anchor
	47	—	403	—	403
		—	275	—	Kreinik gold
		—	Kreinik gold		

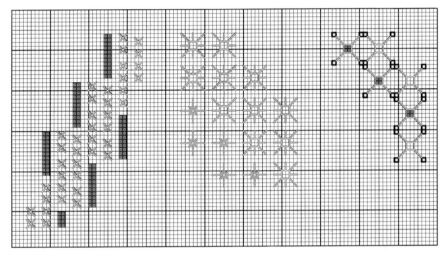

1 To make up: stretch the pieces of linen over each of the card shapes using a double length of sewing thread.

2 Make a 10 cm (4 in) loop of gold braid and sew it to the top of one panel on the wrong side. Hold two of the shapes together and oversew the edges together. Stitch the third panel in place to make a three-dimensional decoration.

3 Cut a 5 cm (2 in) square of card. Mix some black and gold thread and wrap them round the card several times. Tie a loop of gold at the top and cut the threads at the bottom. Wrap a length of gold thread round the tassel to make the waist and tie off. Trim the ends and sew onto the bottom of the decoration.

CHAPTER TWO

TRADITIONAL

The beautiful threads and exquisite fabrics
of these traditional country-style projects are
combined to create delicate yet elaborate
designs which will complement the current
natural look in furnishings and decor.
Allow yourself to be tempted away from the
television and instead try your hand at
a simple lavender bag or a pretty table mat.
The more adventurous embroiderer
could stitch a delicate brooch cushion or one
of the beautiful samplers.

NIGHTDRESS CASE

Match the ribbon in the white crocheted lace edging to the brilliant blue of these pretty cornflowers and bow.

YOU WILL NEED

1.5 m (1²⁄₃ yd) white cotton fabric

10 x 13 cm (4 x 5 in) 12 count waste canvas

tacking (basting) thread

needle

embroidery hoop (frame)

stranded cotton DMC 798, 799, 3347

embroidery needle

tailor's chalk

sewing machine

sewing thread

scissors

60 cm (24 in) white crocheted lace with ribbon insert

pins

WORKING THE CROSS STITCH

Tack (baste) the waste canvas in the centre of the cotton fabric 10 cm (4 in) from one end. Work the cross stitch through the waste canvas using two strands of cotton. The bow should be at the end of the fabric. Manipulate the canvas to loosen the threads and pull them out one by one. Press the embroidery on the reverse side.

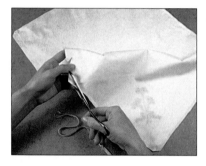

1 To make up: fold the fabric in half crossways and mark the triangular flap with tailor's chalk. With right sides together, stitch round the edge, leaving a gap on one side. Trim the seams and cut across the corners before turning through.

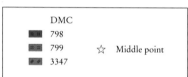

	DMC	
▦	798	
▤	799	☆ Middle point
▨	3347	

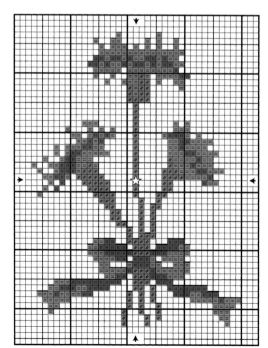

2 Ease out the corners and point of the flap and press on the reverse side. Pin and tack the lace along the edge of the flap and stitch it in place. Fold in the ends of the lace and hand sew. Slip stitch the side seams to finish.

TABLECLOTH AND NAPKIN

This pretty table linen set with its colourful border will make
Sunday lunch a very elegant affair.

YOU WILL NEED

*115 cm (45 in) square of
white 28 count Jobelan for
the tablecloth*

*50 cm (20 in) square of white
28 count Jobelan for the napkin*

tacking (basting) thread

scissors

needle

embroidery hoop (frame)

*stranded cotton Anchor 3 skeins
each of 131 and 133, 1 skein
each of 35, 47, 110, 112,
211, 297*

tapestry needle

pins

sewing thread

sewing machine

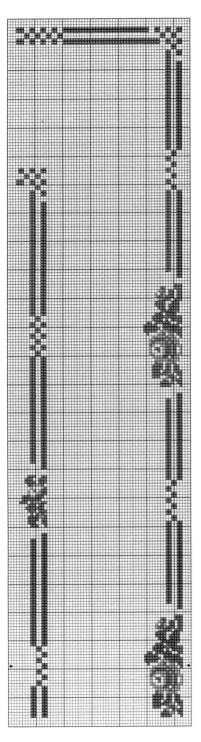

TABLECLOTH

WORKING THE CROSS STITCH

Fold the fabric in half and tack (baste) a guideline about 20 cm (8 in) along one fold to mark the centre on each side. Tack a line across one of these sides, 16 cm (6¼ in) from the edge, as a starting-point. Work the cross stitch using two strands of cotton over two threads.

1 To make up: the chart shows one half of one side. Repeat the design on the other side, keeping the floral motifs facing in the same direction. Continue the cross stitch round the other sides of the tablecloth.

2 Press on the wrong side of the fabric when finished. Trim the fabric to a 95 cm (37½ in) square, mitre the corners and fold over a 2.5 cm (1 in) hem. Stitch close to the turned edge and slip stitch the mitred corners.

NAPKIN

WORKING THE CROSS STITCH

Tack (baste) the centre line as before and mark the starting point 8 cm (3 in) in from the side. Work the cross stitch using two strands of cotton over two threads, repeating the design on all sides.

1 To make up: press the fabric on the reverse side when complete and trim to 45 cm (18 in).

Mitre the corners and fold over a 2 cm (¾ in) hem. Finish in the same way as the tablecloth.

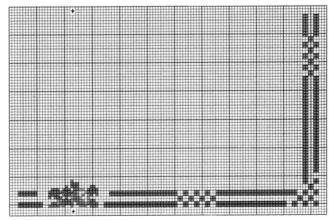

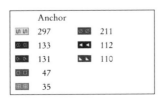

	Anchor		
⊡ ⊡	297	⊙ ⊙	211
▨ ▨	133	◄ ◄	112
▧ ◪	131	◣ ◥	110
▣ ▣	47		
▦ ▦	35		

FLORAL TIEBACKS

These tiebacks are quick and easy to make and are ideal for the kitchen or utility room.

YOU WILL NEED

*1.5 m (1²⁄₃ yd) of
8 cm (3 in) raw linen band,
Zweigart E7272*

scissors

tacking (basting) thread

needle

tapestry needle

*stranded cotton DMC 517, 518,
553, 554, 561, 562, 563, 741*

pins

four 2.5 cm (1 in) brass rings

WORKING THE CROSS STITCH

Cut the linen band into four equal pieces. Tack (baste) guidelines across one of the bands to mark the centre and work the cross stitch using two strands of cotton over two threads. Turn the band round and repeat the design at the other end.

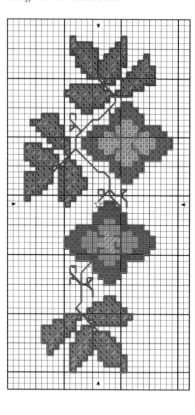

DMC	
▬	517
▦	518
▶◀	553
○○	554
◥◥	562
▱◱	563
╱╱	741
	Backstitch
▬	561
▬	553
▬	517
☆	Middle point

1 To make up: press the band on the reverse side and fold over 5 mm (¼ in) at each end. Fold in the corners to make a point, then pin and tack. Finish a plain piece of linen band in the same way: this will form the backing.

2 Pin the tieback and its facing together, with the raw edges to the inside. Sew a decorative cross stitch every 1 cm (½ in) along the border to join the two pieces together. Slip a brass ring between the layers at each point and sew cross stitches on the point and at either side to secure. Make a second matching tieback in exactly the same way.

HERB BOX AND POT STAND

Keep the herb box on the windowsill filled with fresh herbs. The special heatproof glass inside the pot stand frame will protect the design.

HERB BOX

YOU WILL NEED

60 cm (24 in) of 10 cm (4 in) wide plain bleached linen, Inglestone collection 900/100

tacking (basting) thread

needle

stranded cotton DMC white, 210, 211, 300, 310, 311, 318, 340, 349, 445, 472, 500, 562, 704, 726, 741, 742, 809, 966, 3607, 3746

tapestry needle

scissors

30 cm (12 in) pinewood box

staple gun

WORKING THE CROSS STITCH

Tack (baste) guidelines across the centre of the linen band in both directions then work the cross stitch design using two strands of cotton over two threads of the linen.

1 To make up: once complete, press the linen on the wrong side and then fit round the box. Turn under the ends and staple them to the back of the box.

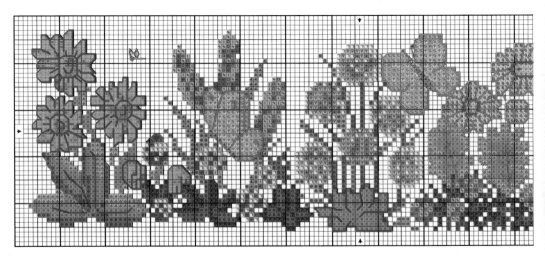

POT STAND

YOU WILL NEED

*23 cm (9 in) square of white
18 count Aida*

tacking (basting) thread

needle

scissors

tapestry needle

embroidery hoop (frame)

*stranded cotton
Anchor 120, 122*

*hexagonal frame,
Framecraft WTS*

WORKING THE CROSS STITCH

Tack (baste) guidelines across the centre of the Aida in both directions. Work the cross stitch using two strands of cotton. Sew the backstitch outlines and press the work on the wrong side. Follow the manufacturer's instructions to fit the embroidery inside the frame. The pot stand has a felt base to protect tables.

DMC		DMC	
⬙⬙	210	⬜⬜	809
⁊⁊	211	⊞⊞	966
▬▬	311	↓↓	3607
⑴⑴	340	↤↤	3746
11	349	◨◨	white
22	310	▽▽	3607 +211
33	300		(1 strand each)
44	318		Backstitch
55	445	——	500
66	472	—◉	300
◪◪	500	——	472
88	562	∞∞	966
99	726	—◉	318
⫿⫿	704	——	310
══	741		
⬚⬚	742	☆	Middle point

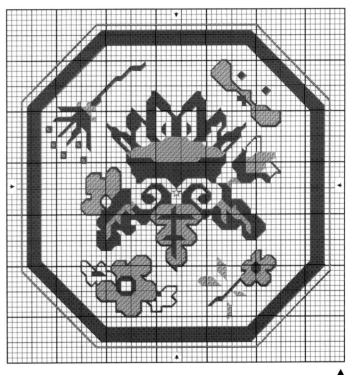

Anchor (in two strands)		Backstitch (in one strand)	Backstitch (in two strands)	
▬▬	122	—— 122	——	120
⁄⁄	120		☆	Middle point

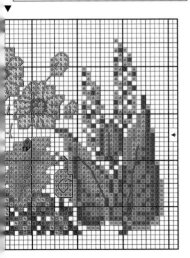

EMBROIDERED SHEET AND PILLOW CASE

This classic bed linen would look superb with a Victorian blue and white wash bowl and jug set on a marble washstand.

YOU WILL NEED

8 cm (3 in) wide Aida band, Fabric Flair BA7349

scissors

sheet and pillow case

stranded cotton Anchor pillow case - two skeins of 130, 132 and one of 134 single sheet - six skeins of 130, five of 132 and three of 134

tapestry needle

pins

sewing thread

sewing machine

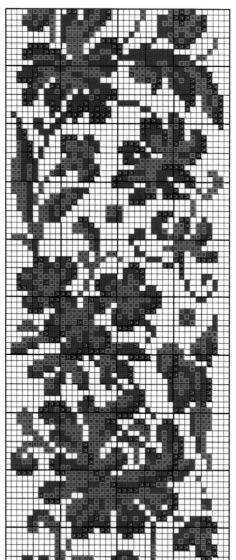

WORKING THE CROSS STITCH

Measure the widths of the sheet and pillow case and cut the Aida band 10 cm (4 in) longer. Work the cross stitch design using two strands of cotton, beginning 5 cm (2 in) from one end.

1 To make up: once complete, press on the wrong side and pin to the sheet or pillow case 6 cm (2½ in) in from the edge. Turn under the ends and stitch the band in place.

Anchor
⊟⊟ 130
▦ 132
▷▷ 134

SPOT MOTIF SAMPLER

Birds, butterflies and flowers were very popular motifs in the nineteenth century, but the pillars make this sampler quite unusual.

YOU WILL NEED

25 cm (10 in) square of Antique Aida 27 count Linda, Zweigart E1235

tacking (basting) thread

needle

embroidery hoop (frame)

stranded cotton Anchor 10, 303, 337, 352, 681, 844, 848, 884

tapestry needle

27 x 30 cm (10½ x 12 in) mount board (backing board)

strong thread

picture frame

WORKING THE CROSS STITCH

Tack (baste) guidelines across the centre of the linen in both directions. Work the cross stitch design using two strands of cotton over two threads.

1 To make up: press the embroidery on the reverse side when complete. Stretch the embroidery over the mount board (backing board) and fit into a picture frame of your choice.

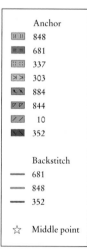

Anchor	
‖ ‖	848
═ ═	681
⠿ ⠿	337
⊳ ⊳	303
◣ ◣	884
▽ ▽	844
╱ ╱	10
◥ ◥	352

Backstitch	
—	681
—	848
—	352

| ☆ | Middle point |

EMBROIDERED COATHANGER

Protect delicate silk negligées and soft woollen sweaters with this pretty padded coathanger.

YOU WILL NEED

30 x 60 cm (12 x 24 in) fabric for the cover

scissors

5 x 25 cm (2 x 10 in) 10 count waste canvas

pins

tacking (basting) thread

needle

stranded cotton Anchor 19, 35, 118, 218, 302, 304

embroidery needle

30 cm (12 in) polyester wadding (batting)

wooden coathanger

sewing thread

double-sided tape

50 cm (20 in) fine cord

WORKING THE CROSS STITCH

Cut the fabric for the cover in half lengthways and the waste canvas into five equal pieces. Pin and tack (baste) a square of waste canvas in the middle of the fabric. Position the other pieces of canvas on either side, leaving a gap of 4 cm (1½ in) between them, and tack securely. Work the cross stitch using two strands of cotton. Once complete, loosen the threads of the waste canvas and pull them out one at a time. Press on reverse side.

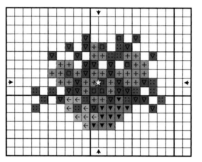

	Anchor			Anchor
	118			302
	35			218
	19			
	304		☆	Middle point

1 To make up: cut the wadding (batting) into four 5 cm (2 in) strips and one of 10 cm (4 in). Wrap the narrow bands round the coathanger and finish with the wider band. Oversew the ends.

2 Trim both pieces of fabric to a width of 11 cm (4½ in), making sure that the cross stitch motifs are along the centre line. With right sides facing and a seam allowance of 1.5 cm (⅝ in), stitch the pieces together, leaving a small gap in the middle for the hook. Press the seam flat and place over the coathanger, feeding the hook through the gap. Turn under the front edge of the fabric, overlap at the bottom of the coathanger and slip stitch.

3 Fold in the fabric at the end of the coathanger and sew tiny running stitches close to the edge. Gather up the stitches and sew in to secure. Cover the hook with double-sided tape. Starting at the curved end, wrap the cord tightly round the hook and sew the end into the wadding of the coathanger to finish.

VICTORIAN SEWING SET

Keep your needles, pins and scissors handy in this pretty sewing set.

NEEDLECASE

WORKING THE CROSS STITCH

Cut a piece of Hardanger 18 x 25 cm (7 x 10 in) and tack (baste) guidelines across the centre in both directions. Leave ten pairs of threads clear on either side of the crossways centre line and work two panels of the cross stitch design. Work the cross stitch using two strands of cotton over one pair of threads. Once complete, pin and tack the ribbon in place between the stitches and sew a large cross stitch where they overlap.

1 To make up: press on the reverse side and iron on the interfacing. Trim the Hardanger and mitre the corners. Fold over the edges and press them flat.

2 Press under a 1 cm (3/8 in) turning all round the lining. Pin and slip stitch the lining to the inside of the needlecase. Fold the felt in half crossways and lay on top of the lining. Stitch down the fold line to complete the needlecase.

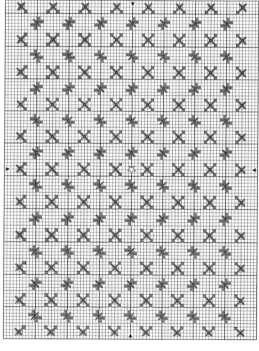

	DMC		Backstitch
7 7	340	—	3685
8 8	341		
▪▪▪▪	3685	☆	Middle point

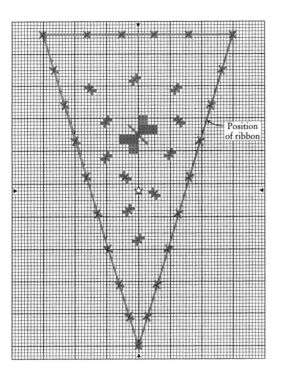

Position
of ribbon

SCISSORS CASE

WORKING THE CROSS STITCH

Work two panels of the cross stitch design using two
strands of cotton over one pair of threads. Press the
embroidery on the reverse side when complete.

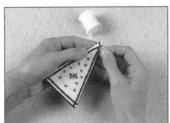

1 To make up: trace the template
and cut four triangles from
thin card (cardboard). Trim the seam
allowance and, positioning the cross
stitch carefully, stretch the
Hardanger over the card using all-
purpose glue. Cover the other two
triangles with lining fabric.

2 Put the lining-covered pieces
together with right sides facing
and place an embroidered panel on
either side with the lining protruding
slightly at the top. Oversew the sides
together securely.

3 Make a tassel by winding a
length of stranded cotton round
a 4 cm (1½ in) square of card
(cardboard). Sew the strip of tassel
onto the point and stitch a 70 cm
(27½ in) length of ribbon to each
side to finish.

SILK TOILET BAG

*The design on this luxurious bag was inspired by
the African violet, a flower much loved by the Victorians.*

YOU WILL NEED

*40 cm (16 in) of eyelet edge
natural linen band, Inglestone
Collection 979/50*

*stranded cotton DMC 341,
550, 744, 3746*

tapestry needle

pins

*35 x 40 cm (14 x 16 in)
burgundy silk dupion
(mid-weight silk)*

sewing thread

sewing machine

*25 x 40 cm (10 x 16 in)
lining fabric*

scissors

needle

six 12 mm (½ in) brass rings

1 m (1 yd) cream cord

WORKING THE CROSS STITCH

Fold the linen band in half lengthways and count the threads to find the centre of the band. Work the cross stitch using two strands of cotton over two threads of linen and repeat the design working out to each end.

1 To make up: press on the reverse side, pin the band to the silk 10 cm (4 in) from the bottom edge and stitch close to the edges. With right sides together, stitch the lining to the silk along the top edge. Press the seam open and stitch the other edges together so that they make a tube shape.

2 Position the seam at the centre back and press open. Stitch along the bottom of the silk, trim and turn through. Turn in the seam allowance of the lining and slip stitch before tucking inside.

3 Cover the rings with buttonhole stitch. Stitch round the top of the bag along the seam line and space the rings evenly before stitching securely in place. Cut the cord in half. Thread the two pieces through in opposite directions and tie the ends together with overhand knots. Unravel the ends of the cord to make pretty tassels.

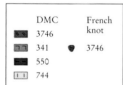

	DMC	French
	3746	knot
	341	● 3746
	550	
	744	

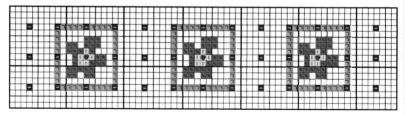

VICTORIAN CUSHION

This design is adapted from some blue and white tiles which were very popular in Victorian times.

YOU WILL NEED

20 cm (8 in) square of Antique white 32 count Belfast linen, Zweigart E3609

tacking (basting) thread

needle

embroidery hoop (frame)

stranded cotton Anchor 1031, 1036

tapestry needle

scissors

50 cm (½ yd) of 90 cm (36 in) navy chintz

tailor's chalk

ruler

sewing machine

sewing thread

1.5 m (1⅔ yd) piping cord

36 cm (14 in) cushion pad

pins

WORKING THE CROSS STITCH

Tack (baste) guidelines across the centre of the linen in both directions and work the cross stitch using two strands of cotton over two threads. Turning the linen through 90 degrees each time, repeat the design in the other three quarters.

1 To make up: trim the linen to within 1.5 cm (⅝ in) of the cross stitch. Turn under 1 cm (⅜ in), mitre the corners and press on the reverse side. Cut two 38 cm (15 in) squares of chintz. Pin and tack the panel in the centre of one piece and slip stitch securely. Draw out sufficient 5 cm (2 in) bias strips on the rest of the fabric to fit round the cushion. Join the bias strips, trim the seams and press open. Cover the piping cord with the strips and tack in place round the edge of the embroidered cushion panel. Stitch. Lay the other panel on top with right sides together and stitch around three sides. Insert the cushion pad and slip stitch the fourth side to complete.

Anchor		
▨▨ 1032	▨▨ 1036	☆ Middle point

TOWEL BORDER

These embroidered Arum lilies, commonly known as cuckoo pint,
look most attractive on a set of pale yellow towels.

WORKING
THE CROSS STITCH

Tack (baste) guidelines in both directions across the centre of the cross stitch panel. Work the cross stitch using two strands of cotton and gold thread. Once complete work the leaf veins using a single strand and the outlines using two strands.

1 To finish: remove the tacking (basting) thread and press on the reverse side.

YOU WILL NEED

white terry hand towel with cross stitch border

tacking (basting) thread

needle

embroidery hoop (frame)

scissors

stranded cotton DMC 310, 680, 725, 727, 783, 895, 3346, 3362

tapestry needle

gold thread DMC Art.284

	DMC
3 3	727
4 4	Art.284
1 1	783
□ □	725
■ ■	895
↓ ↓	3362
∅ ∅	3346
	Backstitch
—	680
—	310
—	895
☆	Middle point

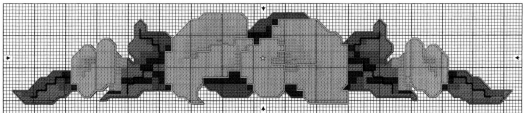

LAVENDER BAG

Tuck this little bag into a drawer to keep your clothes fresh and to remind you of late summer evenings and sweet-smelling flowers.

YOU WILL NEED

30 cm (12 in) of 7.5 cm (3 in) raw linen band with blue scalloped edges, Zweigart E7272

tacking (basting) thread

needle

coton perlé no. 8 DMC 208, 550, 780, 783, 907

tapestry needle

scissors

blue stranded cotton (thread) to match the scalloped edge

sewing thread

dried lavender flowers

WORKING THE CROSS STITCH

Tack (baste) a guideline lengthways down the centre of the band. Tack a second line crossways 6 cm (2½ in) from the top edge. Work the cross stitch over two threads and press on the reverse side.

1 To make up: press under 12 mm (½ in) on each raw edge of the band and sew two rows of running stitch using two strands of blue embroidery thread to secure.

2 Fold the band in half crossways and slip stitch the side seams. Fill with dried lavender flowers or pot pourri and slip stitch the top edges together.

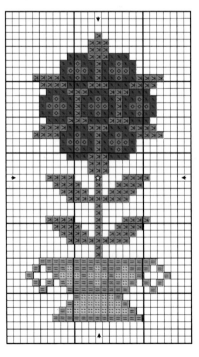

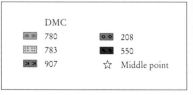

DMC		
══ 780	◐◑ 208	
⊞⊞ 783	◥◣ 550	
⊳⊳ 907	☆ Middle point	

TABLE RUNNER

The linen for the runner is very fine, but the design is fairly quick to sew.

YOU WILL NEED

*50 x 100 cm (20 x 40 in)
36 count white evenweave linen*

tacking (basting) thread

needle

embroidery hoop (frame)

*stranded cotton Anchor
six skeins of 391*

tapestry needle

scissors

sewing machine

sewing thread

WORKING THE CROSS STITCH

Tack (baste) a guideline in one corner, 12 cm (4¾ in) in from each side. This marks the outside edge of the design. Work the cross stitch using two strands of cotton over three threads of the fabric. The second quarter of the design is a mirror image of the first and the second half of the design is a mirror image of the first half.

1 To make up: on completion of the stitching, press on the wrong side. Keeping an equal border all round the embroidery, trim the fabric to 40 x 88 cm (16 x 35 in). Mitre the corners and fold over a 2.5 cm (1 in) hem. Sew close to the fold and slip stitch the corners.

	Anchor
▨ ▨	391
-∎-	Centre lines
☆	Middle point

PICTURE MOUNT

*Personalize the design by adding a name in the panel
below the photograph.*

TRADITIONAL

WORKING THE CROSS STITCH

Mark a 25 cm (10 in) square in the
middle of the canvas and a second
10 cm (4 in) square in the centre of
that one. Tack (baste) guidelines in
the centre of each side of the "mount"
and begin by stitching the bow. The
second side is a mirror image of
the first. Press the embroidery on the
reverse side once complete.

1 To make up: cut out a 10 cm (4 in)
square from the centre of the mount
board (backing board) and stick double-
sided tape round this edge. Cut into each
corner of the centre square on the fabric
and trim. Position the fabric under the
mount and stretch gently onto the tape.
Put more tape round the outside edge.
Mitre the corners and stretch the fabric
onto the tape, checking that the design is
square. Fit into a frame of your choice.

YOU WILL NEED

*35 cm (14 in) square 32 count
natural evenweave linen*

safety ruler

tailor's chalk

tacking (basting) thread

needle

embroidery hoop (frame)

white stranded cotton

tapestry needle

scissors

*25 cm (10 in) square of
mount board (backing board)*

craft knife

double-sided tape

picture frame

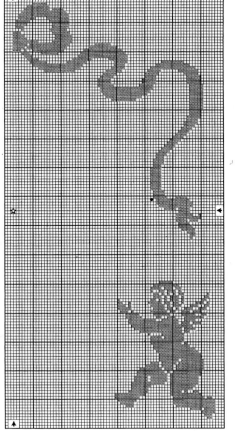

	Anchor
▀▄ ▀▄	white
☆	Middle point

JEWELLERY BOX

*This Charles Rennie Mackintosh design could be adapted to fit any
square or rectangular box you may have.*

YOU WILL NEED

*25 cm (10 in) square gold
32 count evenweave linen*

tacking (basting) thread

needle

interlocking bar frame

tapestry needle

*stranded cotton DMC ecru, 310,
645, 648
Anchor Marlitt 872*

light gold thread DMC Art.282

*gold thread Glissen gloss luster
numbers 02 and 03*

*balger cord Kreinik 105C and
225C*

scissors

double-sided tape

polyester wadding (batting)

wooden box

*1 m (1 yd) of 15 mm (⅝ in)
corded ribbon*

WORKING THE CROSS STITCH

Tack (baste) guidelines in both
directions across the centre of the
linen. Work the cross stitch using
two strands of cotton and single
lengths of cable. Press the design
on the reverse side when complete
and trim to 3 cm (1¼ in) larger
than the box.

	DMC		Anchor Marlitt		Kreinik Balger
	310		872		105C
	Ecru		Glissen Gloss		225C
	645		Gold #02	☆	Middle point
	648		Gold #03		
	Art 282				

1 To make up: cut a square of wadding (batting) and stick it to the lid of the box. Put double-sided tape round the side of the lid and stretch the linen onto it, folding in the corners neatly.

2 Put more double-sided tape round the side of the lid and stick the ribbon down to cover the raw edges. Fold over the end and stick down.

FLORAL TRAY

This delightful tray has a glass inset to protect the embroidery.

YOU WILL NEED

*30 cm (12 in) square of
cream 28 count Cashel linen,
Zweigart E3281*

tacking (basting) thread

needle

embroidery hoop (frame)

*stranded cotton DMC 347,
500, 646, 648, 918, 919, 948,
3047, 3768, 3815*

tapestry needle

*24 cm (9½ in) wooden tray,
Framecraft WSST*

strong thread

WORKING
THE CROSS STITCH

Tack (baste) guidelines in both directions across the centre of the linen. Work the cross stitch using two strands of cotton and press on the reverse side when the design is complete.

1 To make up: stretch the embroidery over the supplied mount board (backing board) and assemble the tray according to the manufacturer's instructions.

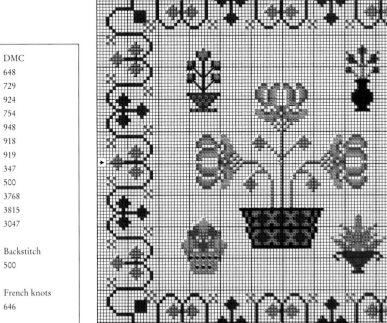

DMC
⁷⁷ 648
ˢˢ 729
924
++ 754
¹¹ 948
918
919
347
500
3768
3815
3047

Backstitch

— 500

French knots

● 646

☆ Middle point

EMBROIDERED
SLIPPERS

A plain pair of slippers can be made special with this pretty rose motif.

YOU WILL NEED

pair of black velvet slippers

*two 9 cm (3½ in) squares of
14 count waste canvas*

*Anchor Nordin 22, 35,
47, 244, 246, 306, 365, 9046*

tapestry needle

thimble

steam iron

WORKING THE CROSS STITCH

Position the waste canvas on the front
of the first slipper and tack (baste) in
place. Find the centre point of the
canvas and begin stitching the design.
The stitches are worked through the
velvet only, using a thimble for ease.

1 To make up: the second slipper
design is a mirror image of the first.
When both are complete, pull the canvas
threads out one at a time. Steam the front
of the slippers to even out the stitches.

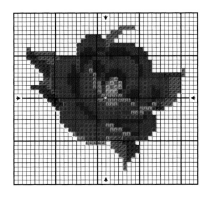

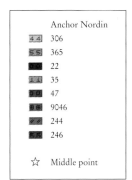

	Anchor Nordin
4 4	306
5 5	365
	22
1 1	35
	47
	9046
	244
	246
☆	Middle point

PRAM QUILT

Children can learn basic colours and numbers using this cleverly designed bright and cheerful quilt.

YOU WILL NEED

61 cm x 76 cm (24 in x 30 in) Anne fabric, Zweigart E7563

embroidery hoop (frame)

stranded cotton DMC 310, 349, 550, 608, 700, 702, 741, 781, 783, 791, 793, 898, 972

tapestry needle

51 x 64 cm (20 x 25 in) medium weight iron-on interfacing

61 x 76 cm (24 x 30 in) cotton lining fabric

61 x 71 cm (24 x 28 in) 4oz wadding (batting)

pins

sewing machine

sewing thread

scissors

needle

3 m (3¼ yd) of 7 mm (¼ in) ribbon

	DMC		DMC		DMC	Backstitch	French knots	
▦	898	⹀	791	⌃⌃	702	—— 898	♥	310
○○	310	⤬⤬	793	ᴋᴋ	781	—— 791	♥	898
⊙⊙	349	▷▷	550	✕✕	783	—— 741		
⌑⌑	608	∥∥	741			—— 781		
╲╲	972	и и	700					

WORKING
THE CROSS STITCH

Cross stitch the border design
inside each square, then find the
centre and work the numbers and
motifs as shown.

1 To make up: iron the
interfacing to the wrong side.
Lay the Anne fabric and lining down
with right sides together. Lay the
wadding (batting) on top and pin
through all the layers.

2 Stitch round the sides close to
the cross stitch, leaving a small
gap for turning. Trim the excess
fabric, turn the quilt through and
ease out the corners. Slip stitch the
gap and press the seams gently.
Attach a 15 cm (6 in) piece of ribbon
at the corners of each square, sewing
through all the layers to give a
quilted effect. Sew or tie the ribbon
into a small bow to finish.

121

BROOCH CUSHION

Keep your brooches safe by pinning them to this delicate cushion.

YOU WILL NEED

*two 20 cm (8 in) squares of
white 36 count evenweave linen*

tacking (basting) thread

needle

embroidery hoop (frame)

*stranded cotton DMC 221,
223, 224, 225, 501, 502, 503,
832, 834, 839, 3032, 3782*

tapestry needle

80 cm (32 in) wine piping

pins

sewing machine

sewing thread

scissors

20 cm (8 in) cushion pad

WORKING THE CROSS STITCH

Tack (baste) guidelines in both
directions across the centre of the
cross stitch panel. Work the cross
stitch using a single strand of cotton
over two threads of linen.

1 To make up: tack the piping round
the edge of the embroidered panel,
overlapping the ends of the piping at one
corner. With right sides together, stitch
round three sides of the cushion, close to
the piping. Trim the seams and corners,
then turn through. Press the cushion
cover and insert the pad. Slip stitch the
gap to finish.

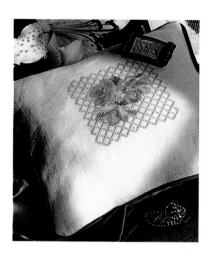

	DMC
▬▬	501
1 1	502
1 1	503
2 2	221
3 3	223
4 4	224
5 5	225
7 7	839
9 9	832
II II	834
○ ○	3032
✕ ✕	3782
☆	Middle point

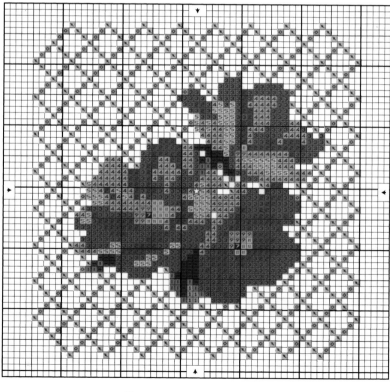

GREETINGS CARD

The card makes a present in itself for a special friend.

WORKING THE CROSS STITCH

Tack (baste) the fine calico to the back of the silk and fit into a hoop. Tack the waste canvas onto the middle of the fabric, keeping the canvas in line with the grain of the fabric. Mark the centre of the canvas. Stitch the design using two strands of cotton. When complete, fray and pull out the canvas threads one at a time. Press on the reverse side and trim to fit behind the opening.

1 To make up: stick tape round the inside edge of the opening and position the embroidery on top. Stick the backing card in position. Use double-sided tape to assemble because glue tends to buckle the card.

YOU WILL NEED

20 cm (8 in) square of fine calico

20 cm (8 in) square of cream silk dupion (mid-weight silk)

tacking (basting) thread

needle

embroidery hoop (frame)

13 x 15 cm (5 x 6 in) 14 count waste canvas

stranded cotton DMC 221, 223, 224, 744, 3362, 3363

embroidery needle

scissors

craft card with an 8 x 12 cm (3 in x 4¾ in) aperture (opening)

double-sided tape

DMC	
224	3363
223	3362
221	
744	☆ Middle point

TRADITIONAL

HANDKERCHIEF CASE

No more scrabbling in the drawer, this pretty and practical pouch will keep all your hankies tidy.

YOU WILL NEED

two 53 x 20 cm (21 x 8 in) pieces of white 36 count evenweave linen

tacking (basting) thread

needle

embroidery hoop (frame)

stranded cotton DMC 221, 223, 224, 225, 501, 502, 503, 832, 834, 839, 3032, 3782

tapestry needle

pins

sewing machine

sewing thread

scissors

1 m (1 yd) wine coloured piping

WORKING THE CROSS STITCH

Tack (baste) a guideline crossways 10 cm (4 in) from one end of the linen. Mark the centre of this line and begin the cross stitch. The bottom of the design is the side nearest the raw edge.

Work the design using a single strand of cotton over two threads of linen. When the embroidery is complete, press on the reverse side. A magnifying glass might help.

	DMC		DMC
██	501	5 5	225
1 1	502	7 7	839
1 1	503	9 9	832
██	221	II II	834
3 3	223	○ ○	3032
4 4	224	× ×	3782

☆ Middle point

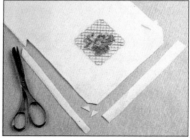

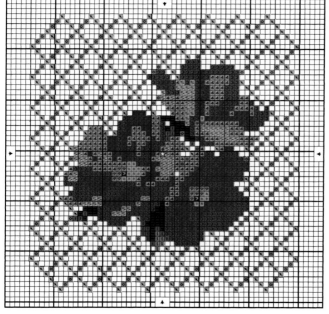

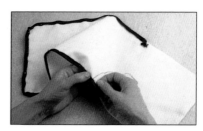

1 To make up: pin the two linen panels together with the embroidery to the inside. With a 2 cm (¾ in) seam allowance, sew all round leaving a gap on one side for turning. Trim the seams and across the corners, then turn through.

2 Fold the panel in three and tack along the fold lines. Pin the piping to the inside of the front flap and down both sides as far as the second fold line. Turn under the ends and slip stitch the piping in place. Slip stitch the side seams to complete the case.

BAND SAMPLER

*Enjoy stitching these ornate and colourful bands, then select
your own initials to embroider at the bottom.*

YOU WILL NEED

*25 x 50 cm (10 x 20 in) cream
28 count Cashel linen, Zweigart
E3281*

tacking (basting) thread

needle

rotating frame

*stranded cotton DMC 224, 225,
312, 347, 3328, 3362, 3363,
3722*

tapestry needle

*30 x 50 cm (12 x 20 in) cream
cotton lawn*

pins

sewing thread

scissors

two wooden hanging bars

50 cm (20 in) red cord

WORKING THE CROSS STITCH

Tack (baste) a guideline crossways, 8 cm (3 in)
from one end of the linen. Begin 5 cm (2 in) in
from the side and work down the chart using two
strands of cotton over two threads. Select your
own initials and stitch them at the bottom of the
sampler. Press on the reverse side when complete.

DMC					
▬▬	347	◈◈	312	╱╱	225
▦▦	3362	✕✕	3363	◣◣	3328
▷▷	224	▰▰	3722	☆	Mid point

1 To make up: pin the
lining to the linen
with the embroidery facing
in and stitch down both
sides close to the cross
stitch. Trim the seams and
turn through.

2 Press the panel and
fold the ends over the
wooden bars. Turn under a
small hem and stitch
securely. Tie the cord to
the top bar and tuck the
ends inside the hem.

GIFT TAG

This gift tag would also look very pretty hanging from the wardrobe door key.

YOU WILL NEED

8 cm (3 in) square of 18 count Rustico, Zweigart E3292

stranded cotton DMC 500, 550, 552, 554, 3363, 3364, 3820

tapestry needle

15 cm (6 in) square of natural handmade paper

craft knife

safety ruler

scissors

all-purpose glue

single hole punch

two reinforcing rings

	DMC
▨▨	552
⬚⬚	554
▶▶	3820
◉◉	3363
✕✕	3364

	Backstitch
—	550
—	500

| ☆ | Middle point |

WORKING THE CROSS STITCH

Beginning in the centre of the canvas, work the cross stitch design using two strands of cotton, and the backstitch using a single strand.

1 To make up: cut two tag shapes out of the handmade paper, and with the craft knife, cut an opening in one. Stick the embroidered panel in the window and trim the edges of the fabric. Glue the back of the label in place.

2 Once the glue has dried, punch a hole at the end of the tag and stick the reinforcing rings on either side. Plait a length of dark green, gold and purple threads together and loop through the hole to finish the tag.

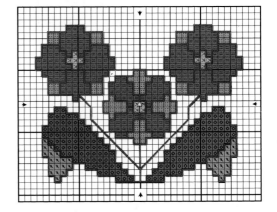

COTTAGE GARDEN TEA COSY

Traditional china teapots need a little help to keep the tea warm.
This padded tea cosy is just the job.

YOU WILL NEED

30 x 40 cm (12 x 16 in) antique
white 28 count evenweave linen

tacking (basting) thread

needle

embroidery hoop (frame)

stranded cotton DMC 341,
352, 372, 422, 433, 435, 451,
543, 666, 725, 746, 776,
778, 825, 828, 899, 951, 986,
989, 3346, 3348, 3726, 3746,
3766, 3799, black

tapestry needle

scissors

30 x 40 cm (12 x 16 in)
lining fabric

30 x 40 cm (12 x 16 in)
wadding (batting)

pins

sewing machine

sewing thread

80 cm (32 in) cord

WORKING THE CROSS STITCH

Tack (baste) guidelines across the centre of the linen in both directions and work the cross stitch using two strands of cotton over two threads. Work the paving slabs using two strands of 433 and all other backstitch using a single strand of cotton. The half cross stitch is also worked using a single strand of cotton (3348). Press on the reverse side when complete.

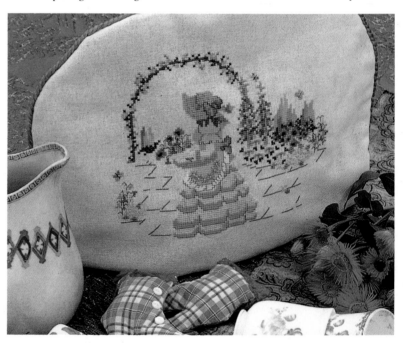

1 To make up: enlarge the template and cut out the front panel from embroidered linen. You will also need a back in linen, two lining pieces and two pieces of wadding. Put the embroidered linen and one piece of lining together with right sides facing and place the wadding on top. Pin the layers together along the straight edge, then tack and stitch. Repeat with the other pieces.

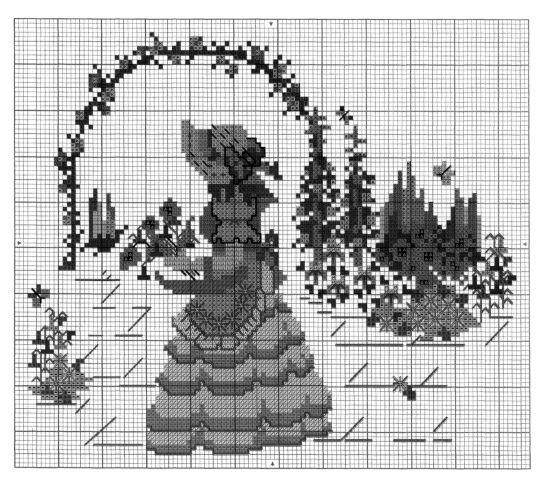

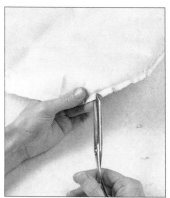

2 Turn the wadding to the inside, pin the panels, right sides facing, and stitch the curved edge. Trim, and notch the curves.

3 Turn through to the right side and press lightly. Slip stitch the cord in place, making a loop for a handle in the middle.

DMC		
═ ═ 341	↓ ↓	3346
⋮⋮ ⋮⋮ 352	← ←	3726
▶ ▶ 372	▽ ▽	3746
○ ○ 422	ℚ ℚ	3766
✕ ✕ 433	△ △	310
▽ ▽ 435	▬ ▬	3348
╱ ╱ 543		
╲ ╲ 666		Backstitch
И И 725	——	451
∧ ∧ 746	══	776
✕ ✕ 776	━━	3726
✕ ✕ 778	——	3746
◙ ◙ 825	——	989
÷ ÷ 828	——	3799
○ ○ 899	——	433
⊥ ⊥ 951		
◨ ◨ 986	☆	Middle point
▣ ▣ 989		

PIN CUSHION

This design may look complicated, but it is easy if you work the floral design first and then fill in the tartan background.

YOU WILL NEED

20 cm (8 in) square of ivory 18 count Aida

tacking (basting) thread

needle

interlocking bar frame

stranded cotton Anchor 2, 43, 110, 112, 210, 226, 235, 268, 291, 337, 340, 403

tapestry needle

scissors

15 cm (6 in) square backing fabric

pins

sewing machine

sewing thread

polyester stuffing

40 cm (16 in) purple satin bias binding

WORKING THE CROSS STITCH

Tack (baste) guidelines across the centre of the Aida in both directions and work the cross stitch using a single strand of cotton. Once complete, press lightly on the reverse side and trim the seams to 5 mm (¼ in).

1 To make up: with right sides facing outwards, stitch the backing to the embroidered panel close to the cross stitch, leaving a gap on one side. Use polyester stuffing to fill the pin cushion and backstitch the gap closed.

2 Open out one side of the binding and pin round the underside of the seam. Join the ends of the binding, then tack and sew in position. Fold the binding onto the right side and slip stitch close to the cross stitch to finish.

	Anchor		43		112		340
	2		291		268		
	226		110		337	☆	Middle point
	210		403		235		

TABLE MAT

This versatile mat would look marvellous on any shape or size of table.
You could change the colour of the trellis
to match your own décor.

WORKING THE CROSS STITCH

Tack (baste) guidelines in both directions across the centre of the linen. Beginning in the centre, work one quarter of the design using two strands of Marlitt over three threads. Once complete, turn the fabric through 90 degrees and work the next section of the cross stitch. The design on each quarter is identical and is not a mirror image. Work the other section in the same way.

YOU WILL NEED

50 cm (20 in) square of white
36 count evenweave linen
tacking (basting) thread
needle
embroidery hoop (frame)
Anchor Marlitt 816,
852, 879, 897, 881
tapestry needle
scissors
sewing machine
sewing thread

1 To make up: once complete, press on the reverse side with a damp cloth. Trim the linen to 40 cm (16 in) diameter. Turn under a narrow hem and tack in position.

2 Stitch close to the folded edge, slip stitch the corners and tack in position. Press carefully as Marlitt is a synthetic thread and may be damaged by a hot iron.

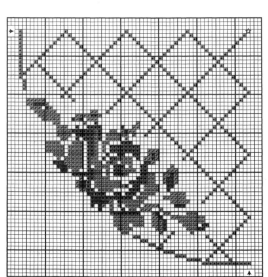

	Anchor Marlitt				
▼	852	▲▲	816	◯◯	879
◢◢	897	▼▼	881	☆	Middle point

SCHOOL SAMPLER

This nineteenth-century sampler is typical of those worked in schools by girls as young as nine or ten as part of their general education.

YOU WILL NEED

40 cm (16 in) square of cream 28 count Cashel linen, Zweigart E3281

tacking (basting) thread

needle

embroidery hoop (frame)

stranded cotton DMC 224, 301, 312, 347, 355, 356, 783, 3362, 3363

tapestry needle

scissors

40 cm (16 in) square of lightweight calico

30 cm (12 in) square of mount board (backing board)

strong thread

picture frame

WORKING THE CROSS STITCH

Tack (baste) guidelines in both directions across the centre of the linen. Work the cross stitch and back stitch using two strands of cotton over two threads of linen.

1 To make up: once complete, press on the reverse side. Lay the lightweight calico on top and then the mount board (backing board). Check the position of the embroidery and make sure the border is straight. Stretch over the mount board. Fit into a frame of your choice.

DMC

347		355		Backstitch
3362		783		—— 347
224		301		
312		3363	☆	Middle point
356				

BIRTH KEEPSAKE

TRADITIONAL

This pretty gift has a practical use as a pin cushion, but could be filled with lavender or potpourri instead.

YOU WILL NEED

15 cm (6 in) square of white 25 count Lugana, Zweigart E3835

tacking (basting) thread

needle

embroidery hoop (frame)

stranded cotton DMC 350, 472, 3326

tapestry needle

118 small pink beads

scissors

15 cm (6 in) square of white backing fabric

sewing machine

sewing thread

two 14 cm (5½ in) squares of wadding (batting)

pins

75 cm (30 in) white crocheted lace edging (dipped in weak tea to colour slightly)

WORKING THE CROSS STITCH

Tack (baste) guidelines in both directions across the centre of the linen. Work the cross stitch using three strands of cotton over two threads. Once complete, sew a bead over the top of each stitch in the pink hearts. Use a double length of thread and begin with a secure knot.

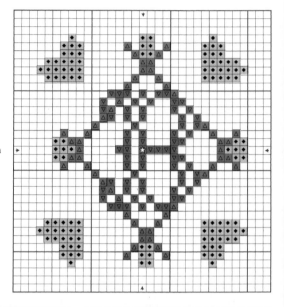

DMC		
▽▽	350	☆ Middle point
△△	472	
◆◆	3326	

1 To make up: block the design if necessary and trim away the excess fabric leaving 4 cm (1½ in) round the cross stitch. Cut the backing fabric to match and stitch the embroidery and backing fabric together with right sides facing, leaving a gap along one side. Trim the seams and across the corners.

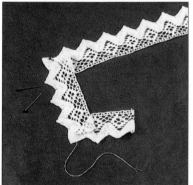

2 Tuck the wadding (batting) into the cushion and slip stitch to close. Mitre the corners of the lace one at a time by folding and stitching diagonally on the wrong side. Each side should be about 13 cm (5 in) long. Join the lace ends and pin round the cushion 1 cm (⅜ in) in from the edge. Stitch in place.

SEWING BOX

The lid of this box has an inset to fit the padded top and can be stained or painted to suit.

YOU WILL NEED

15 cm (6 in) square of cream 22 count Hardanger

tacking (basting) thread

needle

embroidery hoop (frame)

stranded cotton DMC 725, 726, 783, 3362, 3363, 3364, 3687, 3688, 3689

tapestry needle

11.5 cm (4½ in) blank wooden box

oak woodstain

antique wax

compass cutter

10 cm (4 in) square of mount board (backing board)

scissors

sewing thread

10 cm (4 in) square of foam rubber

all-purpose glue

WORKING THE CROSS STITCH

Tack (baste) guidelines in both directions across the centre of the Hardanger and work the cross stitch using a single strand of cotton over one pair of threads. Stain the wooden box and finish with several coats of wax.

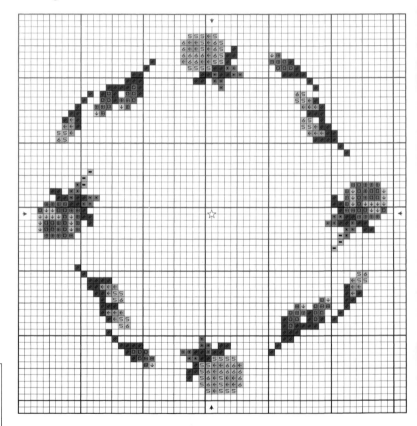

DMC	
5 5	725
6 6	726
0 0	3687
⊞ ⊞	3688
↓ ↓	3689
← ←	783
■ ■	3364
✳ ✳	3363
◢ ◢	3362
☆	Middle point

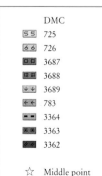

1 To make up: measure the diameter of the inset and cut the mount board (backing board) and foam to fit inside. Keeping the embroidery in the centre, cut the Hardanger 2 cm (¾ in) larger and work a row of small running stitches round the edge.

2 Give the embroidered Hardanger a final press before positioning the fabric face down with the foam and then the mount board (backing board) disc on top of it. Pull up the gathers, check the embroidery is central and stitch the ends securely. Stick in position on the box lid.

TRADITIONAL CHRISTMAS STOCKING

*Hang this beautiful brocade stocking on the fireplace
and who knows what Santa might bring?*

WORKING THE CROSS STITCH

Tack (baste) guidelines across the
linen band as shown and stitch a motif
in each space, staggering them
diagonally. Work the cross stitch using
three strands of cotton over two
threads of linen. Add a strand of
blending filament with the green and
pink threads before stitching.

DMC	
◦◦	Kreinik fine braid gold 102
▦	3052 + Blending filament 045
═	99 + Blending filament 093
■	3802
☆	Middle point

1 To make up: draw out seven threads
near the top and bottom edge of the
linen band. Using three strands of 3802,
twist groups of three threads as shown to
make a decorative border.

2 Scale up the template and cut two
pieces each out of brocade and
lining. With 2 cm (¾ in) seam allowances,
stitch the lining pieces together with right
sides facing. Trim the seams and snip into
the curves. Make the stocking in the same
way but with a 1.5 cm (⅝ in) seam
allowance. Turn through and fold the top
edge over 5 cm (2 in).

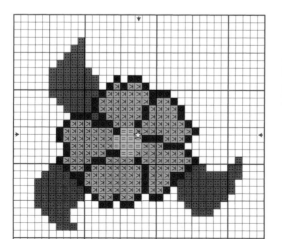

3 Make a tab using a piece of brocade 8 x 20 cm (3 x 8 in). Fold lengthways and stitch, then turn through and press with the seam in the middle of the reverse side. Fold the tab in half and pin onto the back seam of the stocking and sew securely. Fold over 1 cm (³⁄8 in) at the top of the lining and tuck inside the stocking. Pin and tack in position 5 cm (2 in) down from the top and slip stitch. Pin the cuff round the top of the stocking. Slip stitch the back seam and use running stitch to secure the cuff to the stocking.

NEEDLEWORK TIP

Make a small version of
the stocking in
evenweave linen with a
single motif stitched on
the front.

CHRISTMAS DECORATIONS

These Victorian toys are quick and easy to sew on this special vinyl canvas which has a similar weave to Hardanger.

YOU WILL NEED

20 cm (8 in) square of 14 count vinyl weave canvas

stranded cotton Anchor white, 46, 134, 399, 778

fine gold braid Kreinik 002

tapestry needle

scissors

20 cm (8 in) square of thin gold card (cardboard)

all-purpose glue

WORKING THE CROSS STITCH

Stitch the designs onto the canvas using three strands of cotton or the fine gold braid as it comes.

1 To make up: cut round the edge, leaving one row of canvas showing. Oversew the edges with gold braid, except for the rocker on the horse which is oversewn with three strands of blue stranded cotton.

2 Sew a loop of braid onto the saddle, one onto the helmet and one in the middle ie top edge of the drum.

3 Draw round each decoration onto the card (cardboard). Cut out inside the lines and stick the card onto the back of the decoration. Trim away any excess card which is visible on the right side.

	Anchor		134		Kreinik
	399	⁊⁊	778	⊡⊡	fine braid
--	white	₁₁	46		gold 002

CHRISTMAS CARDS

*These snowflakes could be mounted back to back in a card ring
to make an unusual tree decoration.*

WORKING THE CROSS STITCH

Tack (baste) the calico onto the back
of the fabric and fit into a small
embroidery hoop (frame). Tack
guidelines across the fabric to divide
it into six equal segments. Mark the
centre of one strip of canvas and tack
onto the fabric, matching the centres
and the guidelines.

	Anchor		Kreinik fine silver
==	white	▓	braid 001

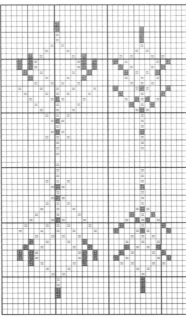

1 To make up: work one of the cross
stitch designs using two strands of
cotton or the fine braid as it comes. Note
that the centre stitch is omitted at this
stage and sewn later. Once complete,
remove the waste canvas carefully, one
thread at a time.

2 Repeat the same
design on each of the
other guidelines to com-
plete the snowflake. Once
all the waste canvas is
carefully removed, stitch
the centre cross.

3 Remove from the
frame, trim to size
and stick behind the
opening of the card.
Stick the flap down to
finish. Make another card
stitching the other
snowflake design onto a
different fabric.

YOU WILL NEED

*15 cm (6 in) square of silk
dupion (mid-weight silk) or
panné velvet*

*15 cm (6 in) square of fine
calico*

tacking (basting) thread

needle

*flexihoop
(small embroidery frame)*

*three 5 x 13 cm (2 x 5 in) strips
of 14 count waste canvas*

vanishing marker pen

tapestry needle

white stranded cotton

fine silver braid Kreinik 001

*silver blending filament Kreinik
001 (optional)*

scissors

*greetings card with a 9.5 cm
(3¾ in) diameter aperture
(opening)*

double-sided tape

CHRISTMAS WREATH PICTURE

Make a fresh holly wreath and decorate with red and orange berries to complement the colours in this embroidery.

YOU WILL NEED

36 cm (14 in) square of cream 14 count Aida

tacking (basting) thread

needle

embroidery hoop (frame)

stranded cotton Anchor white, 47, 214, 228, 236, 313, 314, 1041

tapestry needle

scissors

sewing thread

24 cm (9½ in) diameter mount board (backing board)

WORKING THE CROSS STITCH

Tack (baste) guidelines in both directions across the centre of the Aida and work the cross stitch design using two strands of cotton. Press on the reverse side when complete.

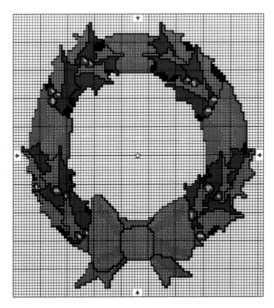

Anchor					Backstitch
	47		236	white	— 236
	214		314		
	228		313	☆	Middle point

1 To make up: trim the Aida to make a 30 cm (12 in) circle with the embroidery in the middle. Using a double thread, sew a row of running stitches round the outside edge. Place the mount board (backing board) on the reverse side and pull up the gathers.

2 Check that the embroidery is straight and central on the mount board then sew in the ends securely. Mount in a picture frame of your choice. Alternatively you could make a fresh wreath on a standard wire frame and attach it to the embroidery with very fine florist's wire.

ANGEL PICTURE

Hang this serene angel above the fireplace at Christmas time and decorate the tree with matching baubles.

YOU WILL NEED

20 x 25 cm (8 x 10 in) ivory 18 count Aida

tacking (basting) thread

needle

interlocking bar frame

˜ tapestry needle

stranded cotton Anchor white, 94, 127, 136, 150, 298, 380, 881, 889, 894, 897, 970

scissors

14.5 x 17.5 cm (5³⁄4 x 6³⁄4 in) mount board (backing board)

strong thread

picture frame

WORKING THE CROSS STITCH

Tack (baste) guidelines in both directions across the centre of the Aida and work the cross stitch using two strands of cotton. Work the backstitch to finish.

1 To make up: press on the reverse side and stretch over the mount board (backing board). Fit into a suitably festive frame of your choice.

Anchor			
– –	white	◇ ◇	894
	94		970/894
= =	127		970
	136		897
	150		
\ \	298		Backstitch
9 9	380	—	380
∧ ∧	881		
✕ ✕	889	☆	Middle point

CHAPTER THREE

FOLK ART

Exotic, unusual and charming designs from
around the world are increasingly
fashionable. Choose from the bright and
richly-coloured embroidery of India
and Pakistan, the earthy colours of Africa
and Mexico or the simple red, blue and white
embroidery of Eastern Europe.
For a more conventional country look,
sew traditional folk-art motifs on rustic
gingham or homespun linen.

SHAKER BOX

These oval beechwood boxes were used by the Shakers to hold all sorts of things. They can be waxed or painted to match the fabric cover.

YOU WILL NEED

20 x 25 cm (8 x 10 in) maroon
18 count Aida

tacking (basting) thread

needle

embroidery hoop (frame)

Anchor Nordin 150, 275, 316

tapestry needle

beechwood box

paper

pencil

scissors

15 x 20 cm (6 x 8 in) thin
wadding (batting)

double-sided tape

60 cm (24 in) of 15 mm (⅝ in)
cream ribbon

60 cm (24 in) of 12 mm (½ in)
navy ribbon

WORKING THE CROSS STITCH

Tack (baste) along the centre line of the Aida in both directions and work the cross stitch using the thread as it comes, then complete the backstitch.

Anchor Nordin	Backstitch
275	—— 316
150	☆ Middle point

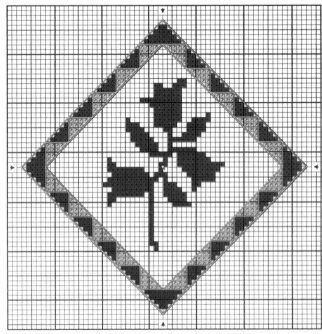

1 To make up: draw round the lid to make a template. Use this to cut out an oval of wadding (batting). Stick it onto the lid. Cut out the cover adding a 1 cm (⅜ in) allowance. Put some double-sided tape round the lid. Centre the design and stretch the fabric down the sides.

2 Put another layer of tape round the rim and stick on the cream ribbon. Trim and butt the ends together.

3 Repeat this process with the blue ribbon, leaving a touch of cream showing. This time turn under the raw end and stick it down.

NINE STAR PICTURE

A simple design inspired by early American patchwork heart and star pictures.

YOU WILL NEED

46 cm (18 in) square of antique white 28 count Cashel linen, Zweigart E3281

vanishing marker pen

tracing paper

pencil

paper scissors

tacking (basting) thread

needle

stranded cotton Anchor 39, 150, 169, 246, 305

tapestry needle

30 cm (12 in) square of mount board (backing board)

strong thread

frame

WORKING THE CROSS STITCH

Mark a 25 cm (10 in) square in the middle of the linen and stitch the border design, sewing 20 hearts across and 24 down. Fold the fabric in half both ways to find the centre and mark with the vanishing marker pen. Work the heart cross stitch pattern within the lines beginning with a heart on the centre mark.

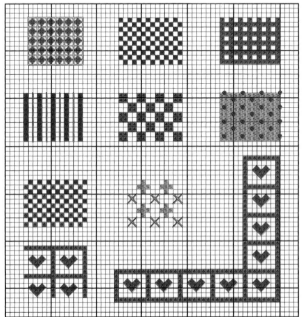

1 To make up: trace and cut out the star template. Place in the centre of the border and draw round it carefully with the pen.

2 Following the grain of the fabric make a second mark on the left 8 cm (3 in) from the centre. Draw round the star template and fill with another cross stitch pattern. Continue in this way, spacing the centres 8 cm (3 in) apart, until all nine stars are complete. Finish the design by stitching a grid of blue running stitch mid way between the stars to make nine equal 8 cm (3 in) boxes.

3 Stretch the linen over the mount board (backing board) and put in a simple frame.

	Anchor		Backstitch
4 4	246	—	39
5 5	305	—	305
6 6	169	—	246
7 7	39		French knots
8 8	150	●	150

UTENSIL BOX

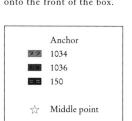

This simple box could be used to store candles, paintbrushes or pens and pencils instead of these kitchen utensils.

WORKING THE CROSS STITCH

Tack (baste) guidelines across the centre of the linen in both directions and work the cross stitch using two strands of cotton over two threads. Press the embroidery on the reverse side when it is complete.

1 To make up: paint the box with two coats of dark blue paint. Allow the paint to dry between coats.

2 Trim the card (cardboard) to fit the front of the box. Stretch the linen over it, mitring the corners neatly, and stick the panel onto the front of the box.

YOU WILL NEED

15 x 20 cm (6 x 8 in) 28 count natural evenweave linen

tacking (basting) thread

needle

embroidery hoop (frame)

stranded cotton Anchor 150, 1034, 1036

tapestry needle

scissors

plain utensil box

dark blue emulsion paint

paintbrush

8 x 15 cm (3 x 6 in) thin card (cardboard)

craft knife

all-purpose glue

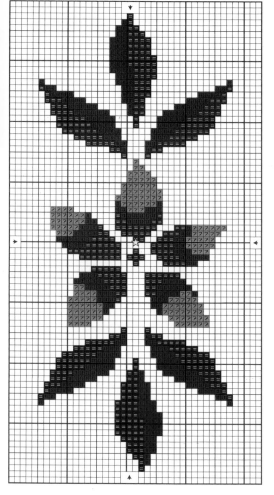

Anchor	
⊿ ⊿	1034
▓	1036
▭	150
☆	Middle point

HEART VINE WREATH

Make the wreath with fresh Virginia creeper or clematis stems and let it dry out under a weight to hold the heart shape.

YOU WILL NEED

20 x 30 cm (8 x 12 in) antique white 28 count Cashel linen, Zweigart E3281

flexihoop (small embroidery frame)

red Anchor Nordin 47

embroidery needle

15 x 23 cm (6 x 9 in) lightweight iron-on interfacing

scissors

pencil

pins

scraps of different red gingham fabrics

sewing thread

polyester stuffing

Virginia creeper or clematis stems

string

WORKING THE CROSS STITCH

Embroider the six hearts onto the linen using one strand of Nordin over two threads of linen, leaving about 2.5 cm (1 in) round each design.

1 To make up: iron on 8 cm (3 in) squares of interfacing to the reverse side and cut out. Draw a heart on each piece, pin to a square of gingham and stitch. Trim the seams, turn through and stuff then slip stitch the gap.

2 Cut eight 60 cm (24 in) lengths of vine. Split the bundle in two and make into a heart shape securing the ends with vine. Wind some more vine round and round the rest of the wreath to hold it together.

3 Sew a 13 cm (5 in) length of embroidery thread through the back of each heart and use it to tie the hearts round the wreath. Add a loop for hanging or fit over a nail.

	Anchor Nordin
⊞⊞	47
	Backstitch
—	47

TRAY CLOTH

This cloth has been specially made for the tray but the design could be adapted slightly to a tray of any size.

YOU WILL NEED

ruler

paper

pencil

scissors

four different "fat quarters" of gingham

medium weight iron-on interfacing

sewing machine

sewing thread

fusible bonding web

stranded cotton Anchor Nordin 144

embroidery needle

cotton lining

nine buttons

WORKING THE CROSS STITCH

Measure your tray and using a scaled up template draw out a paper pattern to fit inside. Adding 1.5 cm (⅝ in) seam allowances all round, cut out a triangle and a strip from each of the four kinds of gingham. Iron interfacing to the reverse side of each piece. With right sides facing, sew each pair of triangles together along the short sides and sew two strips together for each end. Stitch the large triangles together to make a square and sew the strips on opposite sides.

1 To make up: cut four hearts from the bonding web and iron onto the reverse side of different ginghams. Cut out leaving a 5 mm (¼ in) seam allowance. Remove the paper, snip the seams, fold over and press.

2 Position the hearts on the tray cloth and iron again. Sew large cross stitches round each heart and along the seams of the triangles and side panels.

3 With right sides together, sew the lining to the mat leaving a gap. Trim the seams and turn through. Slip stitch the gap and press. Sew a button in the centre and space the other buttons down each of the sides to complete.

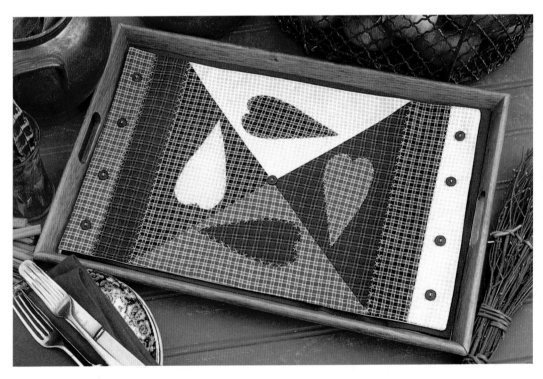

CURTAIN PELMET

These delightful geese would be ideal for a child's bedroom. Simply wrap the fabric round a curtain pole or finish with heading tape.

WORKING THE CROSS STITCH

Measure the width of the window and cut a piece of gingham twice as wide and about 50 cm (20 in) deep. Tack (baste) the squares of waste canvas about 15 cm (6 in) apart along the bottom of the fabric, allowing for the hem and side turnings. Try to position the centre lines of the canvas on the same check each time. Work the cross stitch using three strands of cotton.

1 To make up: once the embroidery is complete, carefully remove the canvas threads one at a time and press the fabric on the reverse side.

2 Finish the raw edges at the side of the pelmet and turn under 5 cm (2 in). Turn up the hem of the pelmet and stitch. Add curtain tape along the top edge or simply wrap the fabric round a curtain pole and adjust the gathers.

YOU WILL NEED

tape measure

red, green and cream gingham

scissors

10 count waste canvas, 10 cm (4 in) square for each motif

tacking (basting) thread

needle

stranded cotton Anchor 386, 879, 1006

embroidery needle

sewing thread

curtain tape (optional)

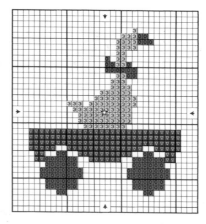

Anchor	
3 3	386
0 0	1006
▽ ▽	879
☆	Middle point

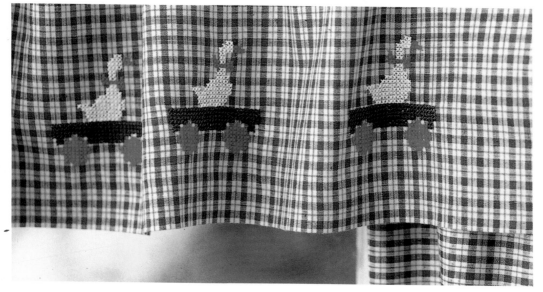

GAME BOARD

*This game board is quite easy to make with only basic
woodworking skills. It is antiqued using crackle varnish and oil paint.*

YOU WILL NEED

*30 x 36 cm (12 x 14 in) gold
32 count evenweave linen*

scissors

tacking (basting) thread

needle

embroidery hoop (frame)

*stranded cotton Anchor white,
44, 170, 211, 403*

tapestry needle

*28 x 51 cm (11 x 20 in) of 5 mm
(¼ in) medium density
fibreboard (MDF)*

*off-white acrylic or emulsion
paint*

paintbrush

ruler

pencil

blackboard paint

*1.6 m (1¾ yd) of 2.5 cm (1 in)
wood edging*

*56 cm (22 in) of 2 cm (¾ in)
wood edging*

fretsaw

wood glue

masking tape

Craquelure, Steps 1 & 2 varnish

raw umber oil paint

soft cloth

antique brown wax

*23 x 28 cm (9 x 11 in)
mount board (backing board)*

safety ruler

craft knife

double-sided tape

WORKING THE CROSS STITCH

Cut the linen in half lengthways. Tack
(baste) guidelines down the centre in
both directions and work the cross
stitch using two strands of cotton over
two threads. Stitch the second piece to
match and press on the reverse side.

1 To make up: paint a 28 cm (11 in)
square in off-white in the middle of
the MDF and allow to dry. Beginning in
the middle of one side, mark every 33 mm
(1¼ in). Repeat on the other edges and
draw out the squares. (There should be an
8 mm (½ in) border all round). Paint the
left hand square black, then paint every
second square black in alternate rows.
When these are dry, paint the remaining
black squares.

2 Cut two 51 cm (20 in) pieces and two
28 cm (11 in) pieces from the 2.5 cm
(1 in) wood edging. Glue these to the side
of the board and hold in place with
masking tape. Cut the narrower strip to fit
inside and stick down across the board.
Paint the completed board with an even
coat of the first varnish and allow to dry
according to the manufacturer's
instructions. Brush on the second varnish
which takes a little longer to dry. Cracks
will appear but may not be obvious as the
varnish is transparent.

3 Next day rub some raw umber oil
paint into the cracks with a soft
cloth and leave to dry. Rub the entire
board with antique brown wax. Measure
the end sections and cut the mount board
(backing board) slightly smaller. Stretch
the embroidery over the mount board and
stick securely inside the end sections
using double-sided tape to complete.

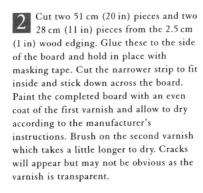

	Anchor		French knots
1 1	170	♥	403
- -	211		
+ +	403	☆	Middle point
1 1	1		
2 2	44		

NAPKIN

*The edge of this napkin has been finished with a pretty
two-colour border to match the heart design.*

YOU WILL NEED

*40 cm (16 in) square of
grey/blue 28 count Jobelan*

sewing machine

sewing thread

scissors

*Anchor Nordin 127, 150, 326,
341*

embroidery needle

tacking (basting) thread

needle

embroidery hoop (frame)

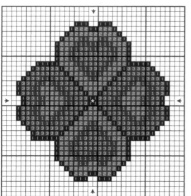

WORKING THE CROSS STITCH

Turn under 5 mm (¼ in) round all sides and machine stitch. Mitre
the corners and turn over a further 5 mm (¼ in). Hold the hem
in place with running stitch in dark blue going over and under
four threads at a time. Complete the border with rust. Tack
(baste) a guideline round one corner of the napkin, 3 cm (1¼ in)
in from the edge. Work the cross stitch over two threads and press.

	Anchor		
1 1	127	3 3	341
1 1	150		
2 2	326	☆	Middle point

HERB DECORATION

This delightful little gingerbread man will cheer up any kitchen and could be filled with a sachet of herbs or potpourri.

WORKING THE CROSS STITCH

Tack (baste) guidelines across the centre of one square of the linen in both directions and work the cross stitch using two strands of cotton over two threads. When complete press on the reverse side.

1 To make up: cut the ribbon in half and pin to the top edge of one square 4 cm (1½ in) apart. Pin the two pieces of linen together with right sides facing, tucking the ribbon inside. Stitch round the sides leaving a 5 cm (2 in) gap at the bottom. Trim the seams and across the corners then turn through.

2 Cut two squares of wadding (batting) the size of the cushion and tuck inside together with a sachet of herbs. Slip stitch the gap closed. Tie a bow for hanging.

YOU WILL NEED

two 16 cm (6¼ in) squares of evergreen 28 count Belfast linen, Zweigart E3609

tacking (basting) thread

needle

interlocking bar frame

stranded cotton DMC 221, 310, 676, 729, 825, 3823

tapestry needle

1 m (1 yd) of 2 cm (¾ in) gingham ribbon

scissors

pins

sewing machine

sewing thread

polyester wadding (batting)

dried herbs or pot pourri

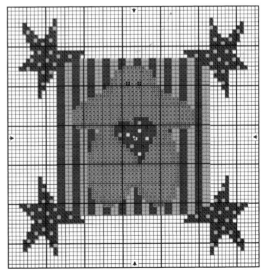

DMC				
⚌ 221	⧓ 676	◥ 825	☆ Middle	
⠿ 3823	◇◇ 729	☐☐ 310	point	

PATCHWORK CUSHION

The motifs on this homespun patchwork cushion are based on nineteenth-century North American samplers.

YOU WILL NEED

nine 13 cm (5 in) squares of different gingham fabrics with approximately 10 squares to 2.5 cm (1 in)

embroidery hoop (frame)

stranded cotton DMC 304, 444, 801, 924, 3821, 3830

embroidery needle

pins

sewing machine

sewing thread

four small pearl buttons

scissors

needle

40 x 60 cm (15 x 24 in) contrast backing fabric

30 cm (12 in) cushion pad

WORKING THE CROSS STITCH

Work the cross stitch using three strands of cotton over each small square. Stitch one orange basket and two of each of the other designs. Once complete, press on the reverse side and lay out the squares on a flat surface to check their positions.

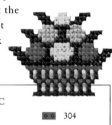

DMC			
≡≡	444	◍◍	304
▩▩	3821	◼◼	801
▶▶	3830	▨▨	924

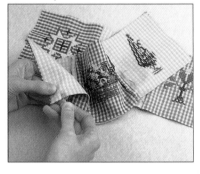

1 To make up: stitch three lots of three squares together with 12 mm (½ in) seam allowances and press the seams open. Pin the rows together matching the seams, stitch and press again. Sew a button at each corner of the centre square.

2 Cut the contrast backing fabric in half to make two 30 x 40 cm (12 x 15 in) rectangles and sew a narrow hem lengthways along one side of each. With right sides together, pin one piece to the left side of the patchwork square and the second piece to the right side. Overlap the hems and sew round all four sides. Trim across the corners and turn through. Tuck the cushion pad inside to complete.

KITCHEN APRON

Everyone will be happy to wear this big, bright apron
with its three cheery gingerbread men.

YOU WILL NEED

large cook's apron

15 x 30 cm (6 x 12 in) 10 count
waste canvas

tacking (basting) thread

needle

coton perlé no.5 DMC 543

embroidery needle

WORKING THE CROSS STITCH

Tack (baste) the waste canvas onto the bib of the apron, positioning it about 8 cm (3 in) down from the top edge. Work the cross stitch as shown through the waste canvas. Once complete remove the tacking thread.

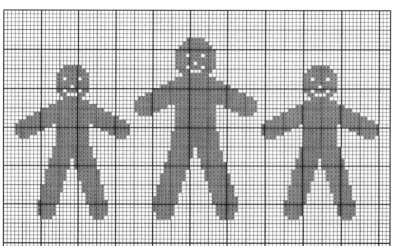

1 To make up: once complete, remove the canvas threads one at a time. You may find it easier to take out the shorter threads first. Press the embroidery on the reverse side.

DMC coton perlé no.5
3 3   543

HAND TOWEL

Make this pretty border to sew on to a plain waffle towel and add your own initials.

YOU WILL NEED

white waffle hand towel

20 x 90 cm (8 x 36 in)
homespun cotton gingham
with approximately 10 square.
to 2.5 cm (1 in)

scissors

tacking (basting) thread

needle

stranded cotton DMC 321,
815, 3808

embroidery needle

pins

sewing machine (optional)

sewing thread

DMC		
	3808	Your
	321	choice
	— 815	

WORKING THE CROSS STITCH

Wash both the towel and the gingham to check for shrinkage. Cut the gingham so that it measures 5 cm (2 in) wider than the towel. Tack (baste) guidelines across the centre of the gingham in both directions and work the cross stitch using three strands of cotton over each square. Stitch your choice of initials first, then work the hearts on either side.

1 To make up: press the embroidery on the reverse side. Trim the long edges so that there is 4 cm (1½ in) on either side of the cross stitch. Press under 12 mm (½ in) on all sides and pin to the end of the towel. Fold the short ends to the back and tack. Hand or machine stitch the gingham close to the edge using matching thread.

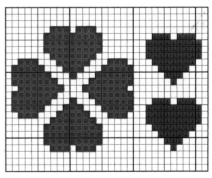

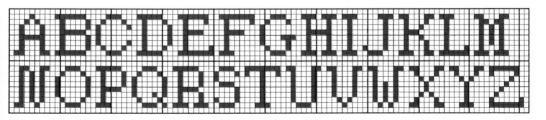

WOODEN SPOON MOBILE

Paint an old wooden spoon and make a charming kitchen decoration with some oddments of gingham and embroidery cotton.

YOU WILL NEED

three 8 cm (3 in) squares of different gingham fabric

three 5 cm (2 in) squares of 14 count waste canvas

tacking (basting) thread

needle

six 10 cm (4 in) squares of contrast gingham

8 x 25 cm (3 x 10 in) fusible bonding web

scissors

Anchor Nordin 13, 134, 281

embroidery needle

sewing machine

sewing thread

polyester stuffing

wooden spoon

pencil

hand drill

yellow paint, Colourman 122

paintbrush

adhesive tape

large eye needle

WORKING THE CROSS STITCH

Tack (baste) the waste canvas onto the small gingham squares and work one motif in the centre of each. Remove the waste canvas one thread at a time once the embroidery is finished and press lightly on the reverse side.

1 To make up: iron fusible bonding web on to the reverse side of the squares and trim them to 5.5 cm (2¼ in). Remove the backing paper and iron the embroidered squares onto three squares of the contrast gingham. Work a row of tiny red running stitches round each small square to secure. Sew the backs onto the cushions with right sides facing, leaving open along one side. Trim the corners and turn through. Fill with stuffing and slip stitch to close.

2 Lay the cushions under the spoon and mark the position of the holes. Drill small holes through the spoon and paint with two coats of yellow paint.

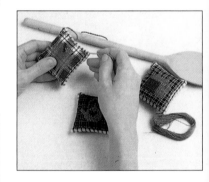

3 Make a 60 cm (24 in) cord with Anchor Nordin 281. Cut it in three equal pieces and tape the ends to prevent them unravelling. Thread a cord through each hole and sew the ends into one corner of each cushion.

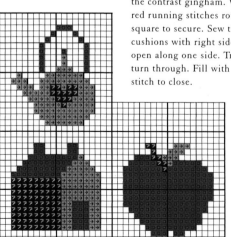

	Anchor
	134
	13
	281

PARTY HORSE

Children love to role-play with this traditional folk art doll who is dressed in her Sunday best and ready for a tea-party.

YOU WILL NEED

20 x 30 cm (8 x 12 in) white cotton fabric

tracing paper

pencil

5 cm (2 in) square of 14 count waste canvas

tacking (basting) thread

needle

stranded cotton DMC 799, 3347

embroidery needle

30 cm (12 in) broderie anglaise

pins

scissors

sewing machine

sewing thread

30 cm (12 in) of 5 mm (¼ in) white ribbon

40 cm (½ yd) of 90 cm (36 in) wide natural linen or fine wool

polyester stuffing

two 5 mm (¼ in) black beads

0.25 m (¼ yd) of 115 cm (45 in) wide blue cotton print

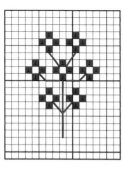

WORKING THE CROSS STITCH

Trace the apron template onto the white cotton. Tack (baste) the waste canvas in the middle of the lower half and work the cross stitch using three strands of cotton. Remove the waste canvas thread by thread and complete the backstitch as shown. Press the embroidery on the reverse side. Pin

the broderie anglaise round the embroidered section of the apron. Fold the apron in half with right sides together and stitch, leaving a gap on one side. Turn through and press. Pin the ribbon across the top of the apron and stitch all round close to the edge.

1 To make up: enlarge the templates and cut out the pattern pieces for the horse. Using 5 mm (¼ in) seam allowance, stitch the heads, ears, arms and legs together in pairs leaving the short straight edges unstitched. Stuff all the pieces except for the ears. Turn the raw edges inside, pinch the bottom of each ear and hand sew on either side of the head seam.

2 For the eyes, stitch on one bead and take the thread through to the other side. Pull it taut to sink the eye slightly and sew on the second bead. Stitch the torso leaving open between the dots and at the top and bottom. Tuck the head inside and slip stitch securely. Attach the arms in the same way, then stuff the body firmly.

3 Pin the legs in place and backstitch through all layers along the bottom of the torso. Cut out the dress bodice and a 20 x 61 cm (8 x 24 in) rectangle for the skirt. Stitch the outer sleeve seam and the underarm seam. Sew a small piece of lace to the neck edge and hem the sleeve ends. Stitch the short ends of the skirt together to form a tube and gather round one end. Pin to the bodice and stitch. Fold under a narrow hem and stitch to complete.

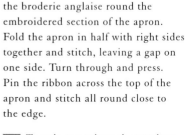

	DMC
▨	799
	Backstitch
—	3347

GUEST TOWEL

Screw two brass hooks to the back of a door or hang this unusual guest towel from a row of wooden pegs.

YOU WILL NEED

white waffle hand towel

30 cm (12 in) homespun check fabric with approximately 10 squares to 2.5 cm (1 in)

scissors

tacking (basting) thread

needle

embroidery hoop (frame)

coton perlé no.5 DMC 311, 400, 469, 726, 814

embroidery needle

pins

sewing machine

sewing thread

40 cm (16 in) woven tape

two pearl buttons

WORKING THE CROSS STITCH

Wash the towel and gingham before beginning to check for colour fastness and shrinkage. Cut the gingham 2.5 cm (1 in) wider than the towel. Fold the fabric in half crossways and mark

this with a line of tacking (basting). Beginning with the red flower, embroider the motifs 5 cm (2 in) up from the bottom of the fabric. Reverse the motifs for the other side.

DMC	Backstitch
726	—— 726
400	—— 311
814	
311	☆ Middle
469	point

1 To make up: with right sides together, stitch the bottom edge of the embroidered panel to the top of the hand towel. Fold and press under a 12 mm (½ in) seam allowance along the top edge. Fold the gingham in half with right sides together, stitch the side seams, then trim and turn through.

2 Slip stitch the folded edge to the back of the towel. Cut the tape in half. Fold into loops and pin the raw edges to each corner of the embroidered panel. Stitch across the bottom of the loop, fold it over on itself and stitch securely. Sew a button to the front of each corner as a trimming.

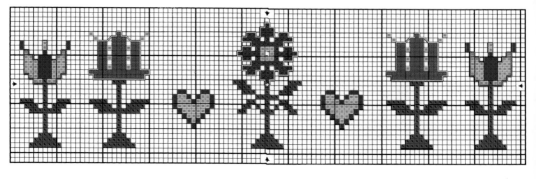

FOLK ART COW

*Children will love this traditional folk art style
cow and the bright colourful border.*

WORKING THE CROSS STITCH

Tack (baste) guidelines across the middle of the Aida in both directions. Begin in the middle and work the cow

picture. Leave two rows of Aida clear all round for the green ribbon. Next, work the patchwork border.

1 To make up: pin the ribbon round the edge of the cross stitch and in the space left round the cow. Stitch the ribbon to the Aida with tiny hem stitches.

2 Cut the mount board (backing board) slightly larger than the outside ribbon edge. Stretch the embroidery over the board and put into a frame of your choice.

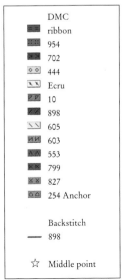

YOU WILL NEED

*36 x 40 cm (14 x 16 in) white
14 count Aida*

tacking (basting) thread

needle

interlocking bar frame

*coton à broder DMC ecru, 10,
444, 553, 603, 605, 702, 799,
827, 898, 954, Anchor 254*

tapestry needle

*1.5 m (1⅝ yd) of 3 mm (⅛ in)
green satin ribbon*

scissors

pins

sewing thread

*30 x 36 cm (12 x 14 in)
mount board (backing board)*

craft knife

safety ruler

strong thread

frame

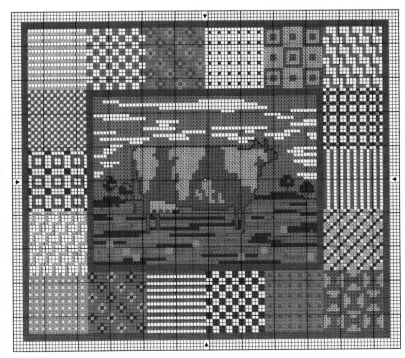

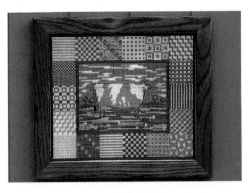

	DMC
⊟⊟	ribbon
∷∷	954
►►	702
◊◊	444
↖↖	Ecru
⬞⬞	10
↗↗	898
↘↘	605
ИИ	603
▲▲	553
◄◄	799
✕✕	827
◠◠	254 Anchor
	Backstitch
—	898
☆	Middle point

HERBS ON A ROPE

*Fill these five lovely bags with cinnamon sticks, chilli peppers
or dried herbs and hang on the kitchen wall.*

YOU WILL NEED

*10 x 15 cm (4 x 6 in) white 16
count Aida*

scissors

stranded cotton DMC 311, 815

tapestry needle

*12 x 20 cm (4¾ x 8 in) dark
blue denim*

pins

embroidery needle

pinking shears

*five 15 x 20 cm (6 x 8 in)
rectangles in different red and
blue checks*

all-purpose glue

sewing machine

sewing thread

*cinnamon, chilli peppers and
other dried herbs*

*1 m (1 yd) heavyweight cotton
cord*

2.5 cm (1 in) brass curtain ring

coarse string

WORKING THE CROSS STITCH

Cut five 4.5 cm (1¾ in) squares out of
the Aida. Work a cross stitch heart in
the middle of each piece using three
strands of cotton and then complete
the red cross stitch.

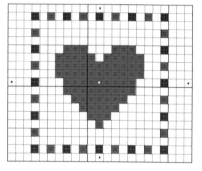

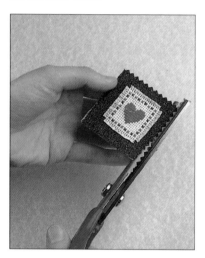

1 To make up: cut five 7 cm (2¾ in)
denim squares and pin the embroidered pieces to them. Work the blue cross
stitch through both layers. Fray the edge
of the Aida squares and trim the edges of
the denim with pinking shears. Glue each
heart motif to the centre of a check
rectangle, 4 cm (1½ in) from the lower
edge. Fold in half so that the heart is on
the inside and stitch the short edges
together. Position the seam at the centre
back and press flat. Stitch along the
bottom edge, trim the corners and turn
through. Trim the tops of the bags with
pinking shears and work a row of running
stitches 4 cm (1½ in) from the top.

DMC		
▦ 815	☆	Middle point
▦ 311		

2 Fill with different herbs, pull up the
running stitches and fasten securely.
Thread the brass ring onto the cord, fold
it in half and bind the top with string to
secure. Tie the bags onto the double string
at intervals using short lengths of string.

EMBROIDERED LAUNDRY BAG

Embroider your own choice of initials in a similar style and make one of these big, useful laundry bags for each member of the family.

YOU WILL NEED

50 cm (20 in) of 6 cm (2½ in) Aida band with red border, Zweigart E7315

stranded cotton DMC 815

tapestry needle

80 x 100 cm (31 x 39 in) white linen or a textured woven cotton

scissors

pins

sewing machine

sewing thread

quilting pencil

needle

2 m (2¼ yd) medium white piping cord

safety pin

comb

WORKING THE CROSS STITCH

Fold the Aida band in half crossways to find the centre and work the cross stitch using three strands of cotton.

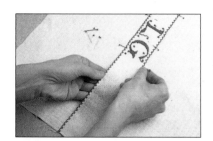

1 To make up: cut the white fabric into two 50 x 80 cm (20 x 31 in) rectangles. Pin, then stitch the band to one piece, 20 cm (8 in) from the lower edge.

2 With the embroidered band on the inside, pin the two pieces together. Starting and finishing 20 cm (8 in) from the top, stitch round the sides and along the bottom. Press the seams open and flatten the corners to make a right angled point at each end of the bottom seam. Measure 5 cm (2½ in) in from each point and mark a diagonal line across each corner. Pin and stitch across the corners to form a flat base.

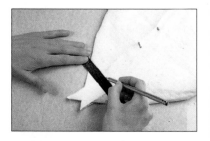

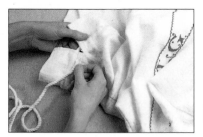

3 Fold over and stitch the seam allowance round both top flaps. Fold in half to the inside and stitch along the edge of the hem. Make a second row of stitching 4 cm (1½ in) up from this to form a drawstring channel. Cut the cord in two and thread through opposite ends of the channel using a safety pin. Knot the two ends of each cord together 8 cm (3 in) from the end. Unravel the ends to form a tassel, comb the ends out and trim neatly.

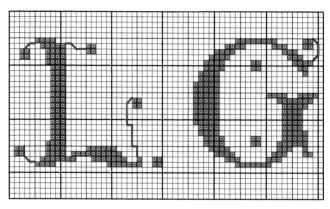

DMC	Backstitch
▫▫ 815	— 815

SWISS ALPHABET SAMPLER

Samplers worked in a single colour were particularly popular in Europe in the nineteenth century.

YOU WILL NEED

30 x 36 cm (12 x 14 in)
white 14 count Aida

tacking (basting) thread

interlocking bar frame

needle

stranded cotton DMC
3 skeins of 304

tapestry needle

23 x 28 cm (9 x 11 in)
mount board (backing board)

strong thread

picture frame

	DMC
▬▬	304
☆	Middle point

WORKING THE CROSS STITCH

Tack (baste) guidelines across the middle of the Aida in both directions and work the cross stitch using three strands of cotton. Work the middle row of letters, then those above and below. Finally stitch the border and corner motifs.

1 To make up: once complete, press on the reverse side and trim any ends of thread so that they do not show through on the right side. Stretch the embroidery over the mount board (backing board) and put into a frame of your choice.

SWISS PILLOWCASE

European countries each have their own particular style of cross stitch.
Plain red on white or cream is typical of Switzerland.

YOU WILL NEED

white Oxford pillowcase

25 cm (10 in) 14 count waste canvas

scissors

tacking (basting) thread

needle

stranded cotton Anchor 47

embroidery needle

NEEDLEWORK TIP

The corner design on
this pillowcase will
depend very much on
the length of the border.
Adapt the chart to suit,
if necessary.

1 Cut 2.5 cm (1 in) strips of
waste canvas and tack (baste)
in position round the border of the
pillow-case, 12 mm (½ in) from the
stitching. Beginning in the centre of
one long side, work the cross stitch
using two strands of cotton.

2 Stop when you are near the
corner and plan the design to
fit the corner based on the cross
stitch chart. Complete the other half
of the side to match and then finish
the rest of the stitching. Press the
pillowcase on the reverse side.

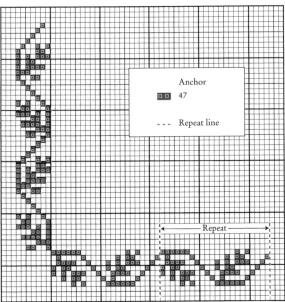

	Anchor
▢▢	47
- - -	Repeat line

Repeat

POTPOURRI SACHET

The beautiful white Austrian lace adds the finishing touch to this charming little cross stitch design.

two 13 x 15 cm (5 x 6 in) pieces of white 14 count Aida

stranded cotton DMC 517, 666

tapestry needle

1 m (1 yd) of 4 cm (1½ in) Austrian lace

tacking (basting) thread

needle

pins

15 cm (6 in) narrow red ribbon

sewing machine

sewing thread

scissors

pot pourri sachet

two 10 x 13 cm (4 x 5 in) pieces of wadding (batting)

	DMC
▦	517
▦	666
	Backstitch
—	666
☆	Middle point

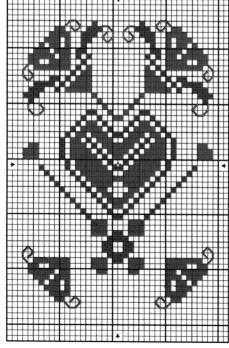

WORKING THE CROSS STITCH

Find the centre of the Aida and work the cross stitch using two strands of cotton and the backstitch using one strand. Press on the reverse side.

1 To make up: gather the lace and pin round the edge of the embroidered panel. Adjust the gathers and tack. Fold the ribbon in half and pin to a top corner with the loop facing inward.

2 With the embroidery and lace to the inside, stitch round three sides. Trim the seams and corners and turn through. Put the pot pourri sachet between the layers of wadding (batting) and insert into the cushion. Slip stitch the opening to finish.

SHELF BORDER

*Red and blue cross stitch is very popular in Eastern Europe where
the carnation is a traditional motif.*

YOU WILL NEED

*7 cm (2³⁄4 in) bleached linen
blue-edged band, Inglestone
collection 950/70*

*stranded cotton Anchor 161,
1006*

tapestry needle

sewing thread

needle

	Anchor
▦	1006
▬	161

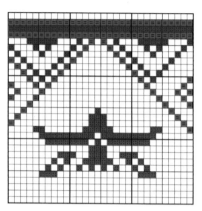

WORKING THE CROSS STITCH

The amount of band and stranded
cotton required will depend on the
length of your shelf.

1 To make up: fold the band in half
crossways and begin stitching the
design in the centre six threads down
from the border. Continue, then repeat
out to both ends of the linen band.

2 Press on the reverse side and stitch
a narrow hem at each end to finish
the raw edges.

BEDSIDE TABLECLOTH

This versatile design could be stitched onto napkins
or on each corner of a much larger tablecloth.

YOU WILL NEED

46 cm (18 in) square of antique white 28 count Cashel linen, Zweigart E3281

tacking (basting) thread

needle

stranded cotton DMC three skeins of 311, one of 3350

tapestry needle

embroidery hoop (frame)

scissors

sewing thread

8 cm (3 in) square of card (cardboard)

WORKING THE CROSS STITCH

Tack (baste) a guideline round a corner of the linen 2.5 cm (1 in) in from the edge. The design begins 90 threads from the corner of the guideline. Work the cross stitch and backstitch over two threads using two strands of cotton.

1 To make up: trim the square to leave a 1.5 cm (⅝ in) seam allowance outside the cross stitch. Mitre the corners and turn a narrow hem. Slip stitch the corners and along the hem.

2 Work the same design in the corner diagonally opposite and press on the reverse side when complete.

3 Wrap blue thread round the card (cardboard) and make four tassels. Stitch these securely to each corner of the mat.

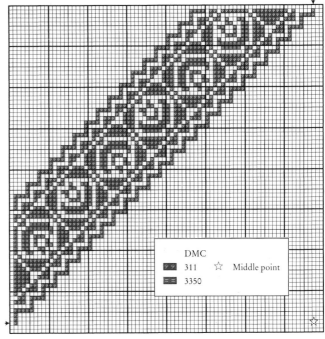

DMC		
♀♀	311	☆ Middle point
==	3350	

CHINESE BOX

*The tiger design on this box is adapted from a cylindrical
Chinese seal from Hong Kong.*

YOU WILL NEED

*30 x 50 cm (12 x 20 in) white
25 count Lugana, Zweigart
E3835*

scissors

tacking (basting) thread

needle

*stranded cotton Anchor 132,
403*

tapestry needle

sewing thread

*20 x 40 cm (8 x 16 in) thin card
(cardboard)*

adhesive tape

*30 cm (12 in) square of blue
lining fabric*

all-purpose glue

WORKING THE CROSS STITCH

Cut a 13 x 25 cm (5 x 10 in) rectangle
of evenweave and tack (baste)
guidelines across the middle in both
directions. Using two strands of cotton
over two threads, outline the tigers in
Holbein stitch (two rows of running
stitch making a solid line). Fill in the
cross stitch and work the Holbein
stitch borders. Press the embroidered
panel on the reverse side. Fold in half
and stitch the short sides together
close to the cross stitch to form a tube.

1 To make up: from thin card (cardboard) cut one 9 x 38 cm (3½ x 15 in)
and one 10 x 19 cm (4 x 7½ in) rectangle.
Curl the long piece round till the two
ends meet and secure with tape. Tuck the
tube inside the embroidered tube. Stick
the raw edges to the inside. Cut a 15 x 22
cm (6 x 8½ in) piece of lining on the bias.
Stitch the two short sides together. Curl
the second piece of card round until it fits
inside the embroidered tube and tape.

2 Put the lining inside the tube and
stretch the fabric to the outside.
Glue a turning of 12 mm (½ in) at the
bottom and the larger area at the top. Cut
two circles out of card to fit the bottoms of
the tubes. Cover the smaller one with
lining fabric and the larger with
evenweave. Oversew the lining circle with
the raw edges facing out and the
evenweave with them facing in.

3 Cut a 2 x 38 cm (¾ x 15 in) strip of
card. Curl it to fit loosely round the
lip of the box. Make a fabric tube from a 6
x 22 cm (2⅜ x 8½ in) piece of evenweave.
Fold it in half and tuck the tube inside.
Stitch round the edge of the card through
both layers. Cover a disc with linen as
before and stitch round the ring, tucking
the raw edges inside. Cut a disc to fit
inside the lid and cover with lining fabric.
Stick the disk on the inside to complete.

Anchor		Backstitch
▨ 132	—	403
☆	Middle point	

INDIAN NECK PURSE

YOU WILL NEED

two 15 x 18 cm (6 x 7 in) pieces of red 20 count evenweave linen

tacking (basting) thread

needle

interlocking bar frame

coton à broder no.16 DMC 321, 444, 552, 700, 796, 907, 943, 947

flower thread DMC 2333, 2531, 2797, 2907, 2917, 2947, 2956

tapestry needle

scissors

50 cm (20 in) of 90 cm (36 in) wide fine navy cotton

sewing machine

sewing thread

easy-turn rouleau maker or bodkin

pins

red wool

8 cm (3 in) square of card (cardboard)

This little bag is typical of those made by the nomadic Banjara people. The design layout was inspired by the wooden architecture in Gujarat.

WORKING THE CROSS STITCH

Experiment by mixing the different colours before working this exciting embroidery project. Subtle changes will occur depending on whether the dark or light thread is on top.

Tack (baste) vertical guidelines corresponding to the panels of the chart on both pieces of linen. The centre panel is worked in coton à broder and the borders in flower threads with each stitch worked over four threads.

Cut several 5 cm (2 in) wide bias strips of the navy cotton and stitch 8 mm ($^3/_8$ in) from the fold, then turn through to make rouleaux. Place the rouleaux in the spaces between the stitching and couch down with groups of two red cross stitches. Leave a border of eight threads round the cross stitch and trim the linen.

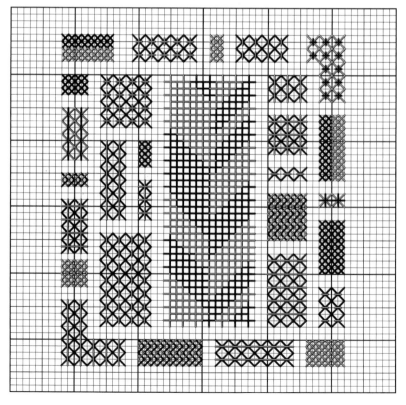

DMC	
—	light areas
—	dark areas

1 To make up: pin and tack each piece onto a 20 x 23 cm (8 x 9 in) rectangle of navy cotton. Machine stitch close to the edge. Mitre the corners of the backing fabric and turn a narrow hem onto the right side of the embroidery. Slip stitch in place.

2 With right sides facing out, oversew the two panels together down the sides and along the bottom.

3 Make three 1 m (39 in) lengths of rouleaux. Thread several strands of red wool through the centre of each to pad. Plait the rouleaux and knot the ends separately. Stitch the rouleaux together 8 cm (3 in) from the end by winding the cottons around the card (cardboard) and making a tassel over each knot. Sew the straps to the bag with cross stitches on the front and the back.

AFRICAN MASK

This stunning mask has been mounted in a long frame to give it the appearance of an African shield.

YOU WILL NEED

30 x 43 cm (12 x 17 in) khaki 28 count Annabelle, Zweigart E3240

tacking (basting) thread

needle

embroidery hoop (frame)

stranded cotton DMC 300, 301, 666, 712, 744, 783, 3371

light gold thread DMC Art.282

tapestry needle

24 x 36 cm (9½ x 14 in) mount board (backing board)

strong thread

picture frame

WORKING THE CROSS STITCH

Tack (baste) guidelines across the middle of the evenweave in both directions. Work the cross stitch design over two threads using two strands of cotton.

Although it will mean that you use all of the gold thread, you will get a more attractive finished piece if you separate the three strands and then put them together again before stitching. Finally, work the backstitch using a single strand of 3371.

1 To make up: press the embroidery on the wrong side. Stretch the fabric over the mount board (backing board) making sure it is centred, and fit into a picture frame of your choice.

DMC			
⹀ ⹀	Art.282	⁄⁄	783
⊞⊞	666	⟍⟍	712
▶▶	3371		
◈◈	300		Backstitch
◥◥	301	—	3371
▽▽	744	☆	Middle point

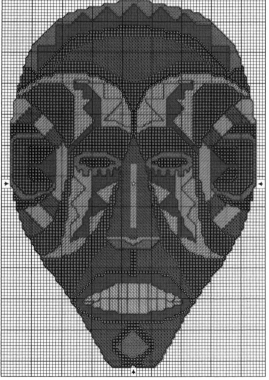

AFRICAN CUSHION

You could make a mini-cushion with this design, but with its fringe border it looks fantastic on a much larger cushion.

YOU WILL NEED

25 cm (10 in) square of 7 count Sudan canvas

rotating frame

tapestry wool Anchor 2 skeins each of 8006, 9490, 9564, 9648, 9800 and one of 9794

tapestry needle

42 x 94 cm (16½ x 37 in) cream furnishing fabric

scissors

pins

1.10 m (1¼ yd) natural fringing

sewing thread

sewing machine

40 cm (16 in) cushion pad

Anchor tapestry wool			
▨▨	9800	▨▨	9794
▨▨	9648	✕✕	8006
▨▨	9564	▨▨	9490
☆	Middle point		

WORKING THE CROSS STITCH

Find the centre of the canvas and work the cross stitch as shown. Once complete, block the design to even out the stitches and trim the seam allowance to 1 cm (³⁄₈ in).

1 To make up: cut a 42 cm (16½ in) square of the cream fabric. Pin and tack (baste) the embroidery in the centre. Pin the fringing round the edge of the cross stitch. Trim and butt the ends of the fringe together taking care that they do not unravel. Tack carefully and stitch. Cut the other piece of cream fabric in half crossways and stitch a narrow hem down one short side of each piece.

2 Overlap the two hems and pin together to make a 42 cm (16½ in) square. Place the two cushion panels together with right sides facing and stitch. Trim the corners and turn through. Unravel the rest of the fringe and make four tassels with the short pieces of yarn. Sew one on each corner of the cushion and insert the cushion pad.

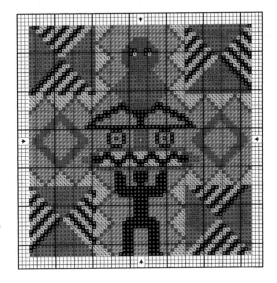

SKETCH BOOK COVER

Cover a sketch book for an artist friend.
The ribbon fastenings help to keep any cuttings or loose sketches safe.

WORKING THE CROSS STITCH

Fold the linen in half crossways and tuck the sketch book inside. Put a pin in to mark the centre of each side of the sketchbook and tack (baste) guidelines to mark the mid-point of the front cover. Work the cross stitch using three strands of cotton over two threads of linen. Once complete, work the backstitch using a single strand of black. Press on the reverse side.

	DMC	
▬▬	310	Backstitch
▦	321	310
⊠⊠	444	☆ Middle point

1 To make up: lay the sketch book on the linen. Check that the embroidery is central and in line with the front cover and mark the corners with pins.

2 Cut across the corners 1 cm (³⁄₈ in)
from the sketch book. Put double-
sided tape all round the inside cover. Hold
the rest of the book upright and stick the
linen onto the back of the cover, mitring
each corner neatly and trimming away
excess fabric if necessary.

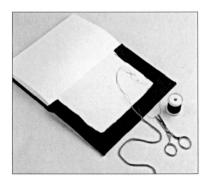

3 Finish the other side in the same
way, making sure that the book
closes easily. Cut the cord in two. Securely
sew one piece in the middle of each inside
cover. Slip stitch the mitred corners
and stick the fly leaves down with double-
sided tape to cover all the raw edges.

BUCKET BAG

*The shape of this bag is based on a shigra basket from Ecuador.
The people there use it to carry fruit and vegetables.*

Anchor Nordin	
———	326
———	341
———	365

WORKING THE CROSS STITCH

This project is unusual because the cross stitch is worked on ordinary canvas. The weave on canvas is quite prominent and it is quite easy to follow the grain. With a little practice you will be able to make evenly sized and spaced stitches.

Cut two 30 x 63 cm (12 x 25 in) rectangles. Fold one piece in half

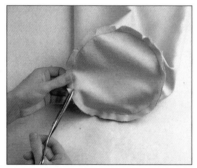

lengthways and mark the fold line with chalk. Work a row of spaced cross stitches in 326, 2 cm (¾ in) either side of the chalk line. Work the single cross stitches and fish motifs between the lines. Work parallel rows of cross stitch 8 cm (3 in) from the raw edge, then finish the other six stitches of the vertical lines to complete the design.

1 To make up: with right sides together stitch the short seams of both panels to form a tube. Cut two 20 cm (8 in) circles from the canvas. Pin one circle to the bottom of each tube, easing the fabric as you go. Tack (baste) and stitch round the base. Snip into the curves and turn the embroidered piece through to the right side.

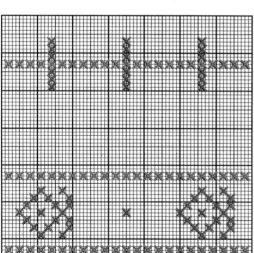

2 Cut the cord in two and pin one piece 6 cm (2½ in) to either side of the centre back seam, with the loop facing towards the bag. Pin the other strap on the opposite side and stitch securely inside the seam allowance.

3 Tuck the lining inside the bag and fold over the top edge of both pieces by about 1.5 cm (⅝ in). Pin and tack the layers together and stitch close to the top edge. Stitch again 5 mm (¼ in) away to finish.

MEXICAN TOY BAG

FOLK ART

Toddlers will be delighted to help tidy their bricks into this big strong bag.

YOU WILL NEED

18 x 46 cm (7 x 18 in) antique white 20 count Bellana, Zweigart E3256

tacking (basting) thread

needle

stranded cotton DMC 300, 310, 349, 603, 704, 806, 972

tapestry needle

80 x 60 cm (32 x 24 in) navy heavyweight twill fabric

scissors

pins

sewing machine

sewing thread

1.60 m (1¾ yd) thick white cord

safety pin

comb

DMC			
	972		310
	704		603
	300		806
	349	Backstitch	
		—	310

WORKING THE CROSS STITCH

Tack (baste) guidelines across the middle of the evenweave. Work the cross stitch design using two strands of cotton over single threads, then work the backstitch. Press gently on the reverse side when complete.

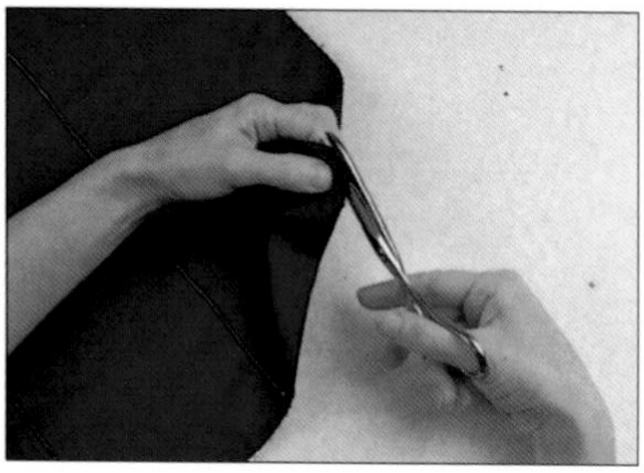

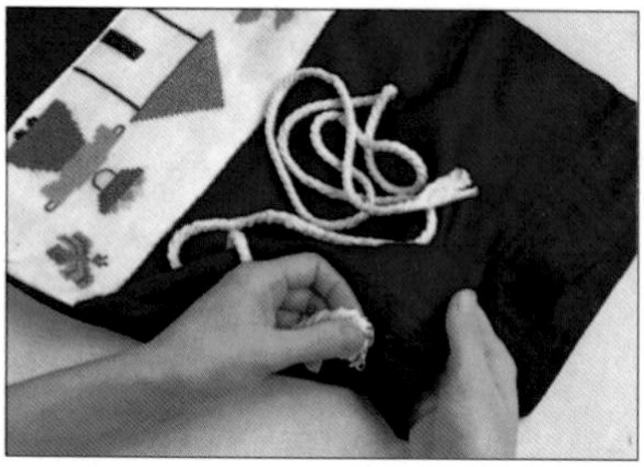

1 To make up: cut the navy fabric in two, crossways. Turn in the long edges of the embroidered panel and pin it 15 cm (6 in) from the bottom of one piece of fabric. Tack (baste) and stitch the two long sides. With right sides facing, pin the pieces together down the sides and bottom. Stitch, leaving a 4 cm (1½ in) gap on both sides 7 cm (2¾ in) from the top. Zig-zag close to the stitching, then trim and turn through.

2 Fold over the top edge and make a 5 cm (2 in) hem. Pin and sew the hem in place and then top stitch 1 cm (½ in) down from the top fold line. Cut the cord in half. Using a large safety pin, thread the pieces of cord through the casing in opposite directions. Tie the ends together 8 cm (3 in) from the end to form a tassel. Unravel the threads, comb them out and trim neatly to finish.

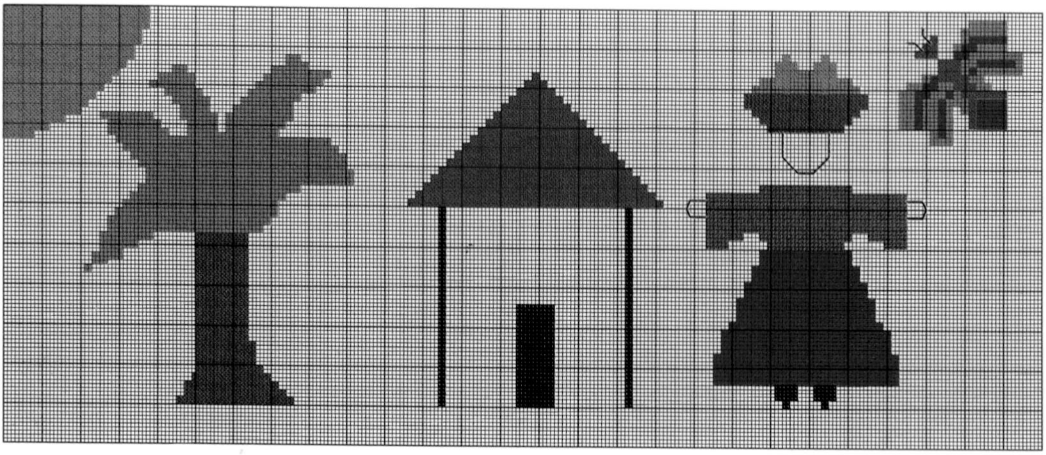

SHOE BAG

Geometric weaving designs can be adapted quite easily into cross stitch.
These stylized animals come from a hammock made in Ghana.

YOU WILL NEED

28 x 66 cm (11 x 26 in) golden tan 28 count Quaker evenweave linen

scissors

tacking (basting) thread

needle

stranded cotton DMC 300, 498, 676, 919, 976

tapestry needle

pins

sewing machine

sewing thread

safety pin

WORKING THE CROSS STITCH

Cut a 5 x 66 cm (2 x 26 in) strip from the fabric for the cord. Fold the larger piece in half both ways and tack (baste) along the folds. Work the cross stitch using two strands of cotton over two threads. Begin at the bottom of the chart, working the cockerel above the crossways tacking. Press on the wrong side when complete.

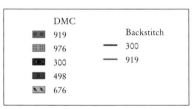

1 To make up: fold the fabric in half with the embroidery facing in. Pin and stitch the two side seams, leaving a 5 cm (2 in) gap on one side 2.5 cm (1 in) from the top. Press the seams open.

2 To make the casing, fold over 5 cm (2 in) at the top. Turn under 12 mm (½ in), then pin and stitch in place. Stitch again close to the top edge.

3 Press the long edges of the reversed fabric strip into the centre. Turn the ends in 12 mm (½ in) and then fold the strip lengthways again. Pin and stitch round all sides. Thread the strap through the casing with a safety pin and stitch the ends together securely. Pull the joined ends through to the other side of the bag to complete the project.

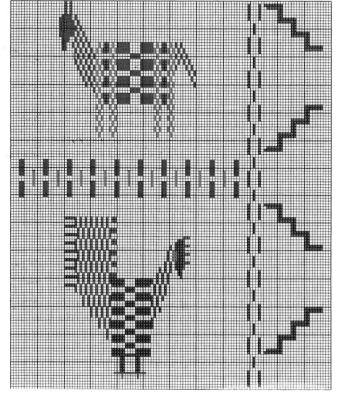

DMC		Backstitch
▦	919	
▦	976	— 300
▨	300	— 919
▨	498	
✕	676	

MEXICAN WALLHANGING

This little hanging was inspired by traditional Mexican God's eyes.
Why not make one or two more to hang alongside it?

YOU WILL NEED

36 cm (14 in) square of 32
count natural evenweave linen

scissors

tacking (basting) thread

needle

small embroidery frame
(flexihoop)

stranded cotton DMC 310, 435,
550, 701, 712, 743, 900

tapestry needle

sewing machine

sewing thread

pins

15 cm (6 in) twig

30 cm (12 in) fine cord

WORKING THE CROSS STITCH

Cut two 18 x 25 cm (7 x 10 in)
rectangles of linen. Tack (baste) a
guideline lengthways down the middle
of one piece. Tack a second line across
the linen, 10 cm (4 in) from the top.
Work the cross stitch and backstitch
using two strands of cotton over two
threads of linen. Press on the reverse
side when complete.

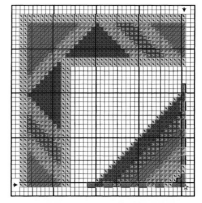

1 To make up: cut two 5 x 13 cm (2 x 5
in) rectangles of linen. Fold each in
half lengthways and stitch a 12 mm (½ in)
seam allowance. Press the seams open
and turn through. Position the seams at
the centre back and press again.

2 Fold the tabs in half with the seam
to the inside and pin along the top
edge, on either side of the embroidered
panel. Pin the two pieces of linen
together, with the embroidery and tabs
to the inside, and stitch along the top and
down both sides. Trim the seams and
corners and turn through.

3 Fray the bottom edge of the hanging
and press on the reverse side. Slip
the twig through the tabs and tie the cord
at each end to hang.

DMC		
435		900
550		
701		Backstitch
712		— 310
743		☆ Middle point

INDIAN MOBILE

Shisha mirrors are traditionally hung to protect against evil, in the belief that any spirit seeing its reflection will be terrified and flee.

YOU WILL NEED

two sheets of dark green stitching paper, Jane Greenoff's Inglestone collection

stranded cotton DMC 3 skeins of 783 and 796, 4 skeins of 911 and 1 skein of 815 and 3765

tapestry needle

scissors

1.5 cm (⅝ in) square of thin card (cardboard)

30 cm (12 in) piano wire

WORKING THE CROSS STITCH

Stitching paper is prone to tear but it can be repaired with sticky tape and the holes repunched with a large needle. Work the different motifs and their mirror images onto the stitching paper using three strands of cotton, and leaving spaces for the shisha mirrors. Apply the mirrors as shown in the techniques section and then fill in any spaces with cross stitch.

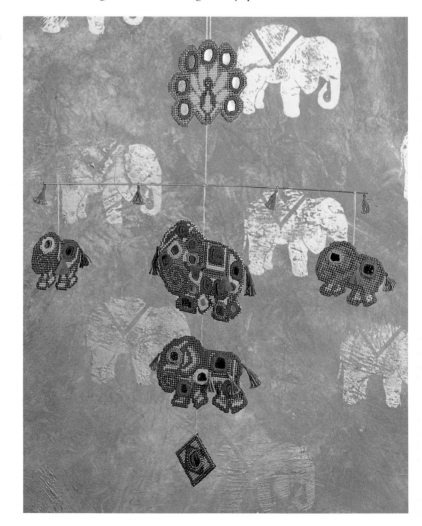

192

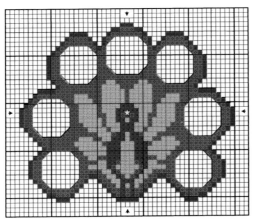

Peacock motif

1 To make up: cut out the different motifs taking care not to snip the stitches. Oversew the two halves together using a single strand of cotton. Separate strands of cotton and make some 1.5 cm (⅝ in) mini-tassels for the elephants. Sew three on each side of the larger elephants and two on the smaller ones. Sew a tassel on one corner of the diamond motif.

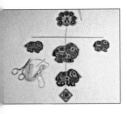

2 Lay out the pieces of the mobile on a flat surface, leaving gaps of about 4 cm (1½ in). Use all six strands of yellow cotton to hold the mobile together. Loop a 20 cm (8 in) length onto the wire. Sew one end to the bottom of the peacock and the other end to the back of the largest elephant. Stitch the other large elephant and the diamond underneath. Loop three strands of cotton over the ends of the wire and stitch the little elephants in place. Complete the mobile with some tassels and stitch a loop for hanging to the back of the peacock.

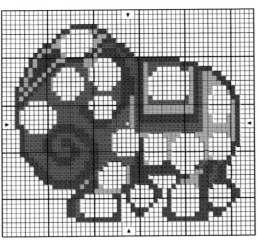

Large elephant motif

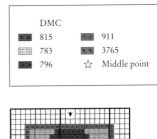

DMC		
815		911
783		3765
796	☆	Middle point

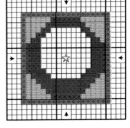

Diamond motif

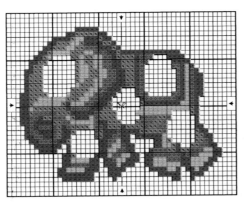

Left: medium elephant   Above: small elephant

193

NAPKIN RING AND TABLE MAT

This elaborate design was adapted from the yoke of a dress stitched and worn by the nomadic Baluchi people of western Pakistan.

YOU WILL NEED

8 x 22 cm (3 x 8½ in) black 18 count Aida for each napkin ring

25 x 36 cm (10 x 14 in) black 18 count Aida for each table mat

tacking (basting) thread

needle

embroidery hoop (frame)

stranded cotton DMC 349, 352, 3731, 3733

tapestry needle

sewing thread

scissors

NAPKIN RING

WORKING THE CROSS STITCH

Tack (baste) a guideline down the centre of the Aida. Using two strands of cotton, stitch three full diamonds with a half diamond at each end.

1 To make up: turn under the top and bottom edges by 5 mm (¼ in) and oversew invisibly on the wrong side. Trim the ends of the band to 5 mm (¼ in) turn under and slip stitch together from the right side.

TABLE MAT

WORKING THE CROSS STITCH

Tack (baste) a guideline round the bottom right hand corner of the Aida 5 cm (2 in) in from the edge. Work three complete diamonds using two strands of cotton.

1 To make up: mitre the corners and turn a small 5 mm (¼ in) hem to the reverse side. Tack in position then machine or hand stitch to finish.

DMC		
═ ═ 349	◇ ◇ 3733	
∷∷ 352	☆ Middle point	
⋈ ⋈ 3731		

INDIAN PICTURE FRAME

Indian embroidery is worked in rich colours and often incorporates different animal motifs. One of the most traditional is the elephant.

YOU WILL NEED

sheet of 7 count plastic canvas

stranded cotton Anchor three skeins of 70 and one each of 150, 254, 258, 304, 307, 1006

tapestry needle

needle

scissors

25 x 30 cm (10 x 12 in) mount board (backing board)

pencil

13 cm (5 in) picture

spray mount

all-purpose glue

small brass ring

sewing thread

WORKING THE CROSS STITCH

The cross stitches in this design are worked with the top stitch direction changing in alternate rows to give the embroidery more texture. Work the cross stitch using all six strands of cotton. You will achieve better coverage of the canvas if the threads are separated and then recombined before stitching.

1 To make up: once the cross stitch is complete, cut out the centre panel and trim the sides. Oversew the edges in two directions to form cross stitches which will cover the edges of the plastic canvas.

2 Mark the size of the frame opening on the mount board (backing board). Spray mount a picture of your choice in position and glue the frame on top. Sew a small brass ring near the top of the frame to hang it by.

Anchor			
⊟⊟	1006	⊼⊼	307
▦▦	70	▷▷	254
◁◁	258	⁄⁄	304
◉◉	150	☆	Middle point

INDIAN MIRROR FRAME

This little mirror frame has been given a rich textured finish with the addition of shisha mirrors and silver beads.

YOU WILL NEED

20 cm (8 in) square of 10 count single thread canvas

stranded cotton Anchor 316, 403, 9046

tapestry needle

four shisha mirrors

double-sided tape

sixteen 5 mm (¼ in) silver beads

11 cm (4¼ in) square of mount board (backing board)

12.5 cm (5 in) square of mount board

30 x 56 cm (12 x 22 in) black cotton fabric

10 cm (4 in) mirror

scissors

pins

sewing thread

needle

5 cm (2 in) black tape

WORKING THE CROSS STITCH

Work the red cross stitch using a double thickness of stranded cotton. Complete the black stitching, leaving space in each corner for the shisha.

1 To make up: stick the shisha onto the canvas with double-sided tape and attach using six strands of black. Sew the beads on with two strands of cotton. Work the orange cross stitch using double thickness stranded cotton.

2 Cover both pieces of mount board (backing board) with black fabric and stick the mirror in the middle of the larger square. Cut out the centre panel of the canvas, leaving 12 mm (½ in) and snip into the corners. Turn under the edges of the embroidered canvas and pin onto the large square of covered mount board. Oversew round all sides.

3 To make the stand, cut a piece of black fabric 2 cm (¾ in) larger than the small covered square. Turn under 1 cm (⅜ in) all round and oversew to the reverse side. Oversew the stand to the mirror frame along one edge and stitch a small piece of tape between the two, at the other end, for support.

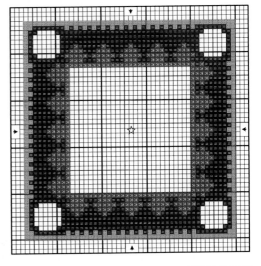

Anchor	▦ 403	⊠ 9046
	▨ 316	☆ Middle point

INDIAN HANGINGS

Indian embroidery often incorporates shisha mirrors to ward off evil spirits but large sequins can be equally effective.

YOU WILL NEED

one sheet of stitching paper,
Jane Greenoff's Inglestone
collection

stranded cotton DMC 436, 469,
738, 744, 783, 796, 806, 824,
915, 917, 918, 920, 922

tapestry needle

1.5 cm (⅝ in) shisha or sequins

2.5 cm (1 in) shisha or sequins

double-sided tape

scissors

pins

sewing thread

needle

small bells

1.5 cm (⅝ in) square of card
(cardboard)

WORKING
THE CROSS STITCH

Stitch the motifs using
three strands of cotton,
leaving spaces as
indicated for the shisha.

These designs are
intended to hang against
the wall. If they are to
hang free both sides will
have to be stitched.

Stitching paper is apt
to tear if stitches are
unpicked but it can be
repaired with sticky tape
and the holes repunched
with a large needle.

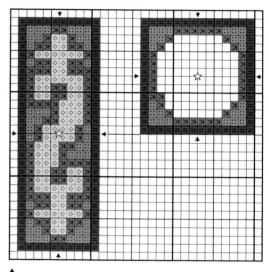

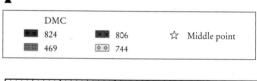

DMC		
824	806	☆ Middle point
469	744	

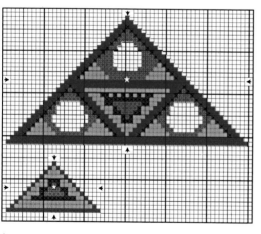

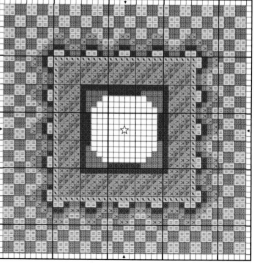

DMC	
915	917
783	☆ Middle point
796	

DMC	
744	738
920	922
436	☆ Middle point
918	

1 To make up: stick the shisha into the spaces and attach as shown in the techniques section. Fill in any spaces round the edge with cross stitch. Cut out the motifs close to the stitching, taking care not to cut any of the threads. Cut a piece of stitching paper to the correct size for each decoration and pin onto the reverse side. Oversew the edges using a single strand of cotton.

2 Assemble the decoration by oversewing the shapes together and winding a thread between the shapes several times to make a "neck" before finishing off. Sew tiny bells on in the same way. Complete the decoration with some tiny tassels, made using single strands of cotton wrapped round the card (cardboard).

CHAPTER FOUR

CONTEMPORARY

These bright and colourful projects
are inspired by lazy summer days, long walks
in flower-filled meadows and holidays
by the deep blue Mediterranean sea.
The delightful modern designs will fit easily
into a contemporary lifestyle.
Beginners can add simple cross stitches to a
waistcoat or bath mat, while more
advanced embroiderers may like to stitch
some huge golden sunflowers on a
tieback or towel.

CUSHION

*This chunky cup design is ideal for conservatory or
kitchen chair cushions.*

YOU WILL NEED

*30 x 46 cm (12 x 18 in)
7 count Sudan canvas*

tacking (basting) thread

needle

rotating frame

*tapestry wool Anchor 8006,
8116, 8306, 8528, 8626, 8986*

tapestry needle

pins

1.5 m (1½ yd) cream piping

sewing machine

sewing thread

*30 x 46 cm (12 x 18 in) cream
backing fabric*

scissors

*25 x 38 cm (10 x 15 in)
cushion pad*

WORKING THE CROSS STITCH

Tack (baste) a guideline in both
directions across the middle of the
canvas. Begin in the centre, working a
cup above and below the horizontal
guideline. Work the cups on either
side, reversing the position of the spots
and stripes. Repeat the wine and green
lines round the design if you wish.

1 To make up: block
the design when
complete. Pin and tack the
piping round the edge of
the cross stitch, over-
lapping the ends along the
bottom. Stitch close to the
piping along that edge.

2 With the embroidery
to the inside, pin and
tack the backing in place.
Stitch round the remaining
three sides. Trim the seams
and corners and turn
through. Insert the
cushion pad and slip stitch
the opening to complete
the project.

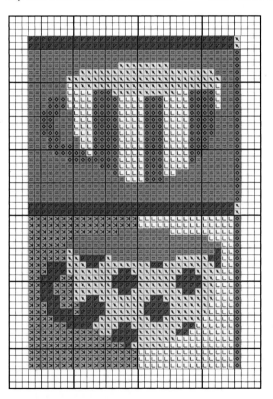

Anchor tapestry wool		
8306		8986
8006		8116
8626		8528

EMBROIDERED DUNGAREES AND HAT BAND

YOU WILL NEED

*denim dungarees with
a plain bib*

*10 x 15 cm (4 x 6 in) 14 count
waste canvas*

pins

tacking (basting) thread

needle

pencil

*stranded cotton Anchor 6, 9, 46,
238, 291, 896*

embroidery needle

straw hat

*60 cm (24 in) of 2.5 cm (1 in)
wide cream Aida band,
Zweigart E7002*

scissors

sewing thread

*These projects match perfectly and make a lovely design for a child's
dungarees and straw hat.*

TO MAKE THE DUNGAREES

WORKING THE CROSS STITCH

The design area for this pig measures 7 x 13 cm (2¾ x 5 in) and is suitable to stitch on age 5–6 dungarees. If you want to embroider a larger area, use 10 count canvas which gives a design size of 10 x 18 cm (4 x 7 in).

Pin and tack (baste) the waste canvas in the middle of the bib. Mark the centre of the canvas with a pencil and work the cross stitch using two strands of cotton (three for 10 count). Once complete, remove the canvas threads one at a time and then press.

Anchor			Backstitch
--	6	22 291	—— 896
11	9	33 46	
11	896	44 238	☆ Middle point

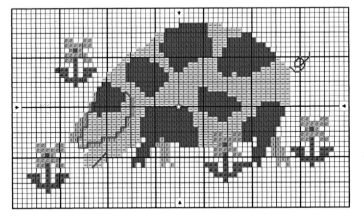

TO MAKE THE HAT BAND

WORKING THE CROSS STITCH

Measure the hat and cut the Aida band 5 cm (2 in) longer. Fold the band in half and put in a pin to mark the centre. Work a flower on the centre line and continue the design out towards each end. Try to finish with flower or the border pattern.

1 To make up: fit the band round the hat. Turn one end in and pin on to of the other end. Slip stitch the ends together. If necessary, secure the band onto the hat by stitching it with prick stitch (tiny running stitches on the front and long stitches on the back).

Anchor	
22	291
33	46
44	238

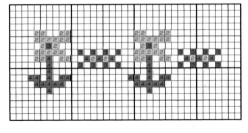

EMBROIDERED BOOK

This little book is made from off-cuts of card (cardboard) and fabrics and contains some small sheets of handmade paper.

YOU WILL NEED

11 x 13 cm (4⅜ x 5 in) gingham

stranded cotton Anchor 352, 890

embroidery needle

25 cm (10 in) square of blue moleskin or denim

scissors

15 cm (6 in) square of floral cotton fabric

15 cm (6 in) square of brown cotton fabric

15 x 30 cm (6 x 12 in) fusible bonding web

all-purpose glue

two pieces of 15 x 18 cm (6 x 7 in) card (cardboard)

masking tape

23 x 38 cm (9 x 15 in) striped cotton

double-sided tape

18 x 33 cm (7 x 13 in) check cotton

pinking shears

5 sheets of hand-made paper 18 x 33 cm (7 x 13 in)

WORKING THE CROSS STITCH

Cross stitch a border round the edge of the piece of gingham. Cut a piece of moleskin to fit inside the border and sew onto the gingham with larger, cruder cross stitches. Iron the fusible bonding web onto the reverse sides of the brown and floral cotton fabrics. Cut out the tree shape and eight petal templates. Remove the backing paper and iron the pieces in place on the moleskin. Sew tiny cross stitches round the shapes. Stitch three crosses along the bottom of the tree and one in the centre of each flower and press on the reverse side. Cut a 12 x 14 cm (4¾ x 5½ in) piece of moleskin and stick to the back of the embroidered gingham with bonding web or glue.

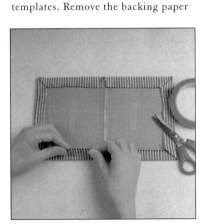

1 To make up: tape the two pieces of card together leaving a 1 cm (⅜ in) gap so that they will fold up like a book. Lay the card in the middle of the reverse side of the striped cotton. Put double-sided tape along the outside edges of the card and stretch the fabric onto the tape, mitring the corners neatly.

2 Cut round the edges of the check fabric with pinking shears to fit onto the inside cover and stick in place. Fold the paper in half crossways and position in the middle of the book. Stitch the pages into the book down the centre fold. Stick the embroidered panel onto the front of the cover to finish.

DECORATIVE MIRROR

This small mirror is just the right size to fit into a handbag and special enough to take with you for an evening out.

YOU WILL NEED

two 15 cm (6 in) squares of 27 count Linda, Zweigart E1235

tacking (basting) thread

needle

small embroidery frame (flexihoop)

fine gold braid Kreinik 002

Anchor Marlitt 845, 870, 1034, 1040, 1140

tapestry needle

craft knife

safety ruler

11 cm (4⅜ in) square of mount board (backing board)

double-sided tape

11 cm (4⅜ in) (approximately) square mirror

scissors

sewing thread

WORKING THE CROSS STITCH

Tack (baste) guidelines across the middle of the linen in both directions. Work the outlines in gold braid over two threads, then complete the mirror's motifs and border using two strands of Marlitt

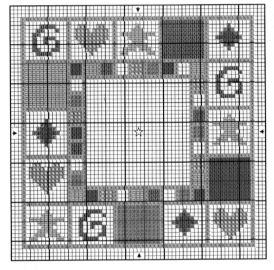

Anchor Marlitt		
⊓⊓ 1034	∃∃	Kreinik
⊏⊏ 845		fine gold
⊏⊏ 870		braid 002
⊏⊏ 1040		
⊠⊠ 1140	☆	Middle point

1 To make up: press carefully on the reverse side, as Marlitt is a synthetic thread. Measure the outside edge of the embroidery, then trim the mount board (backing board) and cut the mirror to size using a glass cutter, or ask a glazier to do it for you. Measure the middle panel and cut the centre out of the mount board.

2 Lay the embroidered linen right side down and cut into the corners of the middle panel. Place the mount board on top and put double-sided tape round the inside edge. Stretch the fabric onto the tape and then lay the mirror on top, face down.

3 Trim the excess fabric to 2.5 cm (1 in) and put more tape round the edge of the mirror. Stretch the fabric onto the mirror back, mitring the corners neatly. Trim the second piece of linen, fold under a small hem and oversew onto the back of the mirror to finish.

GREETINGS CARD

Greetings cards often have a very short life, but this card comes ready mounted and could be displayed in a small frame.

WORKING THE CROSS STITCH

Stretch the linen in a small embroidery frame (flexihoop). Work the cross stitch over two threads in the middle of the linen. Work the stars in backstitch over four threads and then press the linen on the reverse side when complete.

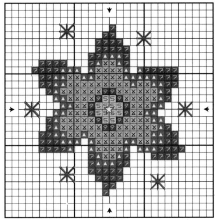

YOU WILL NEED

15 cm (6 in) square of white 28 count Irish linen

small embroidery frame (flexihoop)

Anchor Nordin 119, 127, 134, 144, 290

tapestry needle

10 x 15 cm (4 x 6 in) mount board (backing board)

craft knife

safety ruler

double-sided tape

two different oddments of blue gingham

scissors

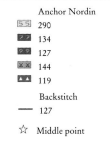

Anchor Nordin
5 5	290
7 7	134
9 9	127
x x	144
▲ ▲	119

Backstitch
— 127

☆ Middle point

1 To make up: cut a 10 cm (4 in) square from the mount board (backing board). Score a line across the remaining strip of board 2.5 cm (1 in) from one end. Stick this end of the strip onto the back of the square to make a simple stand.

2 Cut one piece of gingham slightly smaller than the mount board and stick just above the middle. Repeat with the second gingham then trim the embroidery and stick in place.

TABLE MAT

The colours of the fabric and thread in this geometric design could easily be adapted to suit any room setting.

YOU WILL NEED

*30 x 40 cm (12 x 16 in)
terracotta 28 count evenweave*

tacking (basting) thread

needle

embroidery hoop (frame)

*stranded cotton DMC 310, 743,
712, 3053*

tapestry needle

pins

sewing thread

scissors

WORKING THE CROSS STITCH

Tack (baste) guidelines across the middle of the linen in both directions and work the shapes in cross stitch using two strands of cotton over two threads of linen. Count the threads carefully between the shapes.

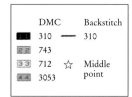

DMC	Backstitch
▨ 310	—— 310
▨ 743	
▨ 712	☆ Middle
▨ 3053	point

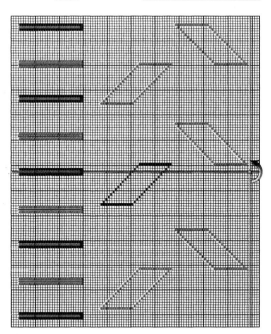

1 To make up: leaving a 5 cm (2 in) tail of threads from each of the side stripes, work the cross stitch and then the backstitch.

2 Press on the reverse side and turn under a small hem down both long sides of the mat. Pin and slip stitch in position.

3 Using the ends of the loose threads as guidelines, fold over a deeper hem at each end. Pin and slip stitch to complete. Press the mat on the reverse side and trim the fringes to 3 cm (1¼ in).

PHOTOFRAME

This frame was inspired by the Art Deco period at the beginning of the twentieth century which brought about the first "modern" designs.

WORKING THE CROSS STITCH

Start in one corner of the linen about 4 cm (1½ in) in from the sides. Work the cross stitch in rows across or down for a smooth finish, using two strands of cotton. Press the embroidery on the reverse side when complete.

YOU WILL NEED

25 x 30 cm (10 x 12 in) white 14 count Aida

stranded cotton Anchor 259, 273, 308, 311, 870, 872, 968, 9159

tapestry needle

18 x 23 cm (7 x 9 in) mount board (backing board)

craft knife

safety ruler

double-sided tape

scissors

76 cm (30 in) of 2.5 cm (1 in) wood strip

hand saw

sandpaper

all-purpose glue

staple gun

masking tape

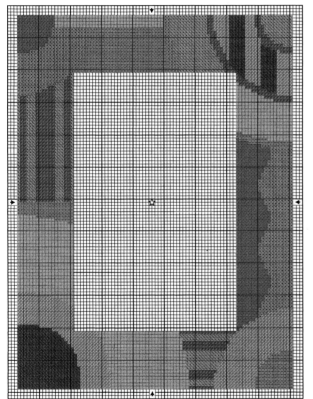

	Anchor
▣▤	308
⠿	259
⊠⊠	9159
◇◇	870
＼＼	311
▥▥	872
／／	968
＼＼	273
☆	Middle point

1 To make up: measure the embroidery, cut a mount exactly the same size and put double-sided tape round the inside edge. Cut into the inner corners of the embroidery and lay the mount on top. Trim the excess fabric and stretch on the tape.

2 Saw two strips of wood to fit lengthways on the back of the mount and two shorter strips to fit in between. Sand the ends and glue in position at the edge of the mount. Insert some staples across the joins for extra strength.

3 Mitre the corners and stretch the fabric onto the back of the frame. Use staples to hold in position and trim away the excess fabric. Cover the raw edges with masking tape. Make a cord using one of the embroidery threads and stick round the front edge of the frame to finish.

TIEBACKS

These big sunflowers stand out beautifully against the dark blue and white gingham fabric.

YOU WILL NEED

1 m (1 yd) of 90 cm (36 in) wide blue and white gingham

scissors

18 x 50 cm (7 x 20 in) 14 count waste canvas

pins

tacking (basting) thread

needle

stranded cotton DMC 300, 301, 400, 433, 742, 743, 904, 906, 938, 977, 986

embroidery needle

tracing paper

pencil

36 x 66 cm (14 x 26 in) medium weight iron-on interfacing

sewing machine

sewing thread

four white "D" rings

WORKING THE CROSS STITCH

If you can buy evenweave gingham, which is produced but is not readily available, work the design directly onto the fabric. Cut the gingham into four 23 x 68 cm (9 x 27 in) pieces. Fold one piece in four to find the centre and open out. Pin and tack (baste) half the waste canvas in the centre of the right hand side. Mark the centre of the waste canvas and work the cross

stitch using two strands of cotton. Once complete, remove the canvas one thread at a time and press the embroidery on the reverse side.

DMC					
▰▰ 300		◣◣ 742		▨▨ 938	
⠿⠿ 301		▽▽ 743		◣◣ 977	
✕✕ 400		⁄⁄ 904		✕✕ 986	
◉◉ 433		◥◥ 906		☆ Middle point	

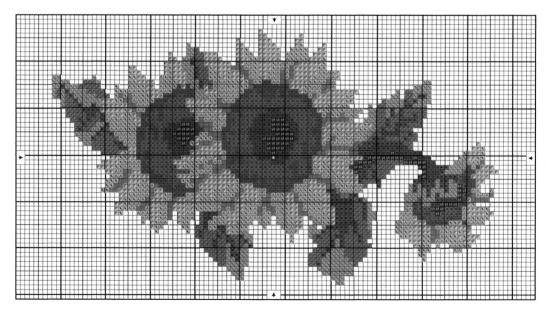

1 To make up: trace and enlarge the template onto tracing paper. Cut out a back and front from the tieback pattern, making sure that the sunflower is positioned correctly. Iron interfacing to the back pattern piece. With right sides together, sew the front and back together along both long sides. Trim the seams and snip into the curves.

2 Turn the tieback through, roll the edges between your thumb and first finger to centre the seams and press on the reverse side. Turn each end over the straight edge of a "D" ring, folding the excess fabric into tucks. Turn under a small hem and stitch securely. Make a second tieback in exactly the same way, stitching a mirror image of the sunflower on the left hand side of the gingham.

TOWEL

This towel is designed to match the sunflower tiebacks.
They would make a co-ordinating set for a plain white bathroom.

YOU WILL NEED

navy blue towel

25 cm (10 in) square of 14 count waste canvas

pins

tacking (basting) thread

needle

stranded cotton DMC 300, 301, 400, 433, 742, 743, 938, 977

embroidery needle

scissors

WORKING THE CROSS STITCH

Pin and tack (baste) the canvas at one end of the towel where you wish to stitch the motif. Work the cross stitch over two pairs of threads using six strands of cotton. You will get a better result if the strands are separated and recombined before stitching. Once complete, fray and remove the canvas threads one at a time. Press lightly with a steam iron on the reverse side, taking care not to damage the towel.

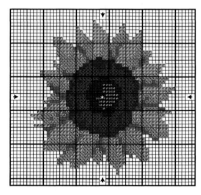

	DMC
▬▬	300
▦▦	301
▶▶	400
✦✦	433
↘↘	742
▽▽	743
и и	938
∧∧	977
☆	Middle point

DAISY CUSHION

The petal colour on this huge daisy could be changed to match a
different check cushion. Choose a dark and light shade of the same colour.

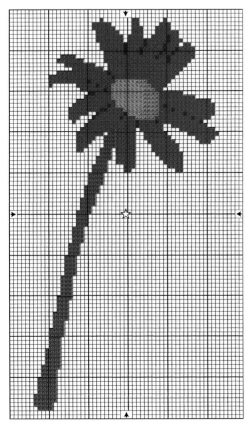

WORKING THE CROSS STITCH

Pin and tack (baste) the waste canvas in the middle of the cushion cover with the opening to the bottom. Fit a large embroidery hoop (frame) on the front of the cushion cover. Mark the centre of the canvas and work the cross stitch using three strands of cotton.

YOU WILL NEED

30 cm (12 in) check cushion cover

15 x 30 cm (6 x 12 in) 10 count waste canvas

pins

tacking (basting) thread

needle

large embroidery hoop (frame)

pencil

stranded cotton Anchor 45, 212, 305, 306, 891, 896

embroidery needle

30 cm (12 in) cushion pad

Anchor	
██	45
33	896
44	306
55	305
66	891
vv	212

1 To make up: once the cover is complete, fray and remove the canvas threads one at a time. Press the embroidery on the reverse side, then turn the cover through and insert the cushion pad to finish.

GARDEN APRON

This big apron, with its large pocket, is ideal for holding small tools and protecting your clothes while working in the garden.

YOU WILL NEED

paper

pencil

90 cm (1 yd) of 115 cm (45 in) wide sand canvas

tailor's chalk

scissors

pins

sewing machine

sewing thread

tacking (basting) thread

needle

safety pin

20 cm (8 in) square of 10 count waste canvas

stranded cotton Anchor 46, 212, 226, 238, 316, 926

embroidery needle

WORKING THE CROSS STITCH

You may find it easier to work the cross stitch after you have made up the apron. Pin and tack (baste) the waste canvas in the middle of the bib. Work the cross stitch and the backstitch details on the plants using three strands of cotton. Then stitch the French knots. Remove the waste canvas before working the rest of the backstitch. Mark the position of the squares and stitch along the grain of the canvas to complete the design.

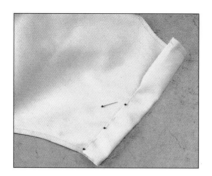

1 To make up: enlarge the pattern pieces and draw round them onto the canvas. Cut out two pockets, one front pattern piece and three 5 x 50 cm (2 x 20 in) strips. Turn over and stitch a small hem along the curved edges, the sides and bottom of the apron. Fold over 12 mm (½ in) along the top edge and then a further 2.5 cm (1 in). Pin, tack (baste) and stitch round all sides of the turning.

2 Fold the strips in half lengthways. Sew 12 mm (½ in) from the raw edge, leaving the straps open at one end, and turn through with a safety pin. Tuck the raw edges inside and press the straps. Pin and tack one strap to either side of the apron and the other one to the top of the bib. Machine stitch in a rectangle to secure the straps. Stitch again for extra strength.

3 Sew the pocket pieces together, with right sides facing, leaving an 8 cm (3 in) gap along the straight edge. Trim and snip the curves, then turn through. Roll the edges between your fingers to make a good curved edge and press. Top stitch the straight edge, pin and tack to the apron and stitch in place. Stitch round the curved edge again for extra strength and sew straight down the centre of the pocket in the same way. Once complete, pin and tack the waste canvas in the middle of the bib.

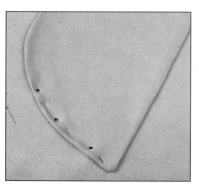

	Anchor		Backstitch		
3 3	926	—	238	☆	Middle point
4 4	316	—	212		
▽ ▽	212		French knots		
↑ ↑	226	🔴	46		

NOAH'S ARK

Noah's Ark is a perennial favourite and this design with its colourful animals and bright border is particularly appealing.

YOU WILL NEED

30 x 36 cm (12 x 14 in) white 22 count Hardanger

tacking (basting) thread

needle

interlocking bar frame

stranded cotton DMC white, 310, 444, 666, 702, 797, 970, 996

tapestry needle

25 x 30 cm (10 x 12 in) mount board (backing board)

strong thread

picture frame

WORKING THE CROSS STITCH

Tack (baste) guidelines in both directions across the middle of the Hardanger. Work the cross stitch using three strands of cotton over two pairs of threads.

1 To make up: once complete, press on the reverse side. Stretch over the mount board (backing board) and fit into a frame of your choice.

DMC		
702		444
970		797
996		310
666		Blanc

Backstitch
— 310

French knots
♥ 310 —

☆ Middle point

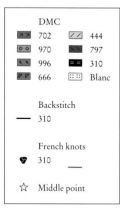

PENCIL POT

*This little bird adds a touch of fun to a plain pencil pot, but could
also be made into a greetings card or miniature picture.*

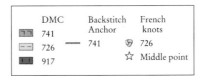

WORKING THE CROSS STITCH

Beginning with the border design,
work the cross stitch and the
backstitch using two strands of cotton
over two threads of linen. Once it is
complete, press on the reverse side and
finish with a French knot for the eye.

	DMC	Backstitch Anchor	French knots
⊓⊓	741		
⊏⊏	726	— 741	◈ 726
⊏⊞	917		☆ Middle point

YOU WILL NEED

*15 cm (6 in) square of white
28 count Irish linen*

*small embroidery frame
(flexihoop)*

*stranded cotton DMC
726, 741, 917*

tapestry needle

*10 cm (4 in) square of
burgundy fabric*

scissors

yellow pencil pot

double-sided tape

1 To make up: cut
the burgundy fabric
to fit the front of the box.
Stick in place with double-
sided tape. Cut the
embroidery slightly
smaller than the fabric and
stick in the middle to
finish.

CONTEMPORARY

CHILDREN'S BADGES

Children love badges to pin onto sweatshirts, hats and bags.
These designs are stitched on plastic canvas and are very easy to sew.

YOU WILL NEED

sheet of 10 or 14 count plastic canvas

Anchor Marlitt 800, 801, 814, 850, 854, 893, 1030, 1056

tapestry needle

scissors

safety pin or brooch pin

WORKING THE CROSS STITCH

All the designs can be worked on 10 or 14 count plastic canvas. The 10 count makes an 8 – 10 cm (3 – 4 in) badge and the 14 count makes one which measures 5 – 7 cm (2 – 2¾ in). Work the cross stitch motifs using two strands of Marlitt on 14 count plastic canvas or four strands on 10 count.

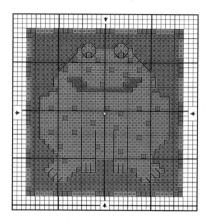

Anchor Marlitt		Backstitch	
1030	850	——	801
1056	893	☆	Middle point
854			

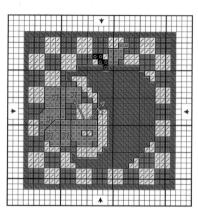

Anchor Marlitt		Backstitch	
1030	801	——	801
1056		——	850
893	☆	Middle point	French knot
800			850

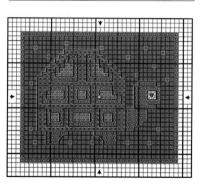

Anchor Marlitt		Backstitch	
1056	800	——	801
814			French knot
850	☆	Middle point	801
854			

220

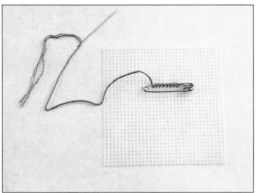

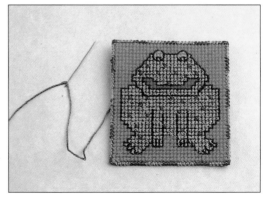

1 To make up: cut each badge out one hole away from the stitches. Cut a second piece of canvas the same size. Oversew a safety pin or brooch pin to the blank piece of canvas.

2 Hold the two pieces together and oversew, using two or four strands depending on the count of the canvas. Slip the ends between the layers and snip.

BATHROOM CABINET

CONTEMPORARY

This fun cabinet was handmade in pine and painted with red and white stripes to match the cross stitch design.

YOU WILL NEED

30 x 40 cm (12 x 16 in) blue 32 count linen

tacking (basting) thread

needle

embroidery hoop (frame)

stranded cotton DMC white, 310, 321, 322, 444, 824, 839, 948

tapestry needle

two pieces of mount board (backing board) each 28 x 38 cm (11 x 15 in)

craft knife

safety ruler

strong thread

panel pins

hammer

WORKING THE CROSS STITCH

Tack (baste) guidelines across the middle of the linen in both directions. Work the cross stitch using two strands of cotton but use only one strand for the backstitch. Press on the reverse side when complete.

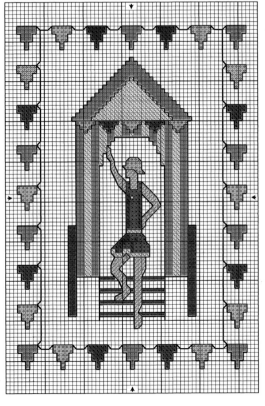

DMC		Backstitch
839	824	— 310
321	948	
322	white	☆ Middle point
444		

1 To make up: cut the mount board (backing board) to fit into the opening in the door. Stretch the embroidery and fit into the door. Place a second piece of mount board behind the embroidery and fix in position using panel pins.

EMBROIDERED LINEN SHIRT

Decorate a plain shirt for a special occasion with this simple and elegant design in glistening embroidery threads.

YOU WILL NEED

plain linen shirt

Anchor Marlitt 864, 1003, 1036, 1040, 1140

tapestry needle

scissors

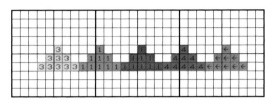

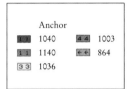

Anchor

■■ 1040		◢◢ 1003	
▦▦ 1140		← ← 864	
▨▨ 1036			

WORKING THE CROSS STITCH

This shirt is made from fabric with quite a prominent, even weave which made it easy to work the cross stitch directly onto the fabric. If you want to work on a finely woven fabric use the waste canvas technique to keep the stitches even.

1 Choose a shirt with a long pointed collar which has the straight grain of the fabric following the outside edge of the collar. Starting 1 cm (³⁄₈ in) in from the edge, work the cross stitch using two strands of cotton. Begin and finish the threads as neatly as possible on the reverse side.

2 Following the same sequence of colours, work a single cross stitch between the buttonholes on the front band of the shirt.

3 Finish the embroidery on the shirt by working the cross stitch design along the edge of the cuffs.

DECORATIVE BATH MAT

This plain cotton bath mat has been stitched with large swirls and cross stitches to co-ordinate with the bathroom accessories.

YOU WILL NEED

natural cotton bath mat

tacking (basting) thread

needle

soft cotton Anchor 11, 13, 228, 242, 305, 307

large sharp needle

scissors

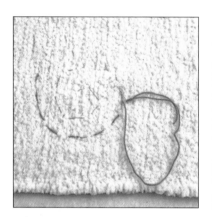

1 Stitching the lines about 2.5 cm (1 in) apart, tack (baste) twelve large swirls spaced evenly over the bath mat. Leave a 5 cm (2 in) end of soft cotton on the reverse side and stitch the spirals using 2.5 cm (1 in) running stitches. When you reach the end of the spiral, work back along the stitching line to fill in the spaces.

2 Work two spirals in each colour and then tie the ends of the cotton together with a secure knot.

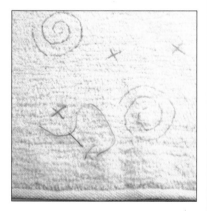

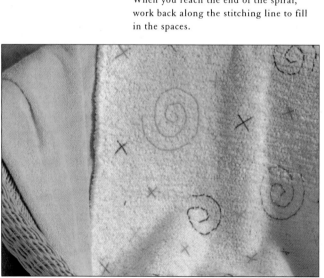

3 Work the cross stitches in between the spirals, beginning and finishing the thread in the same way. Finish the mat with a row of different coloured cross stitches along each end.

PLUM CURTAINS

Linen bands stitched with juicy plums add the finishing touch to these large check cotton curtains.

YOU WILL NEED

8 cm (3 in) bleached linen band, Inglestone Collection 980/80

scissors

tacking (basting) thread

needle

pins

stranded cotton Anchor 69, 70, 72, 212, 373, 905

tapestry needle

pair of green check curtains

sewing machine

sewing thread

WORKING THE CROSS STITCH

The amount of linen band required will depend on the width of the curtains. Cut a piece of linen about 10 cm (4 in) longer than the width of the curtains and fold in half cross-ways. Tack (baste) a guideline down the crease. Measure and mark with a pin every 20 – 25 cm (8 – 10 in) in both directions, keeping the last pins about 15 cm (6 in) from the end of the linen band, then tack guidelines in both directions. The positioning of the motifs will need adjusting depending on the width of your curtains.

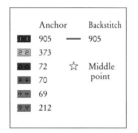

	Anchor		Backstitch
I I	905	——	905
2 2	373		
0 0	72	☆	Middle point
÷ ÷	70		
⋈ ⋈	69		
▽ ▽	212		

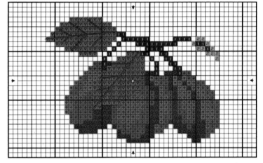

1 Work the plum motifs in the centre of the linen using two strands of cotton over two threads. Once complete, work the backstitch.

2 To make up: pin the linen band along the top of the curtain hem, taking the excess band onto the reverse side of the curtain. Turn under the raw edges and tack in position. Stitch along both sides close to the edge. Press on the reverse side and complete the second curtain to match.

PLUM BOX

*This little painted box has an insert panel in the lid
which is ideal for a small piece of cross stitch.*

WORKING THE CROSS STITCH

Work the cross stitch using a single strand of cotton over one thread of the linen. You will find it easier to work the plum first and then the background.

YOU WILL NEED

*15 cm (6 in) square of white
28 count linen*

*small embroidery frame
(flexihoop)*

*stranded cotton DMC 498,
581, 718, 732, 791, 814, 817,
905, 907, 936, 3721, 3731,
3746, 3810*

tapestry needle

*papier mâché box with insert,
Decorative Arts*

*two shades of yellow acrylic
paint*

sponge

*8 cm (3 in) square of wadding
(batting)*

*8 cm (3 in) square of thin card
(cardboard)*

scissors

double-sided tape

1 To make up: sponge paint the box with the lighter paint and allow to dry. Sponge the second colour on top, allowing the light paint to show through.

2 Press the embroidery on the reverse side. Stretch the linen over the wadding (batting) and card, then fit inside the lid. Secure the insert panel using double-sided tape.

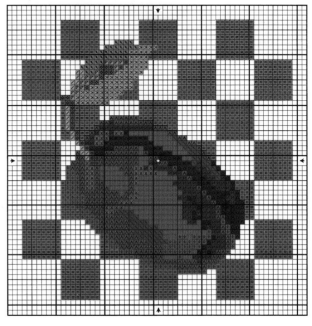

DMC		
══ 3810	⫶⫶ 732	✕✕ 814
▦ 718	⫽⫽ 581	✕✕ 3731
✕✕ 907	◣◣ 817	◼◼ 791
◎◎ 936	ꟽꟽ 498	⹔⹔ 3746
◣◣ 905	▲▲ 3721	☆ Middle point

CLOCK

Navy and cream paint has been cracked with crackle varnish to make an unusual frame for this beautiful Assisi work.

YOU WILL NEED

20 cm (8 in) square of 18 count navy Aida, Zweigart E3793

tacking (basting) thread

needle

Anchor stranded cotton 1223

tapestry needle

scissors

22 cm (9 in) square of 6 mm (¼ in) thick MDF

hand drill with 10 mm (⅜ in) drill bit

1.2 m (1⅓ yd) wood architrave

hand saw

wood glue

masking tape

sandpaper

acrylic paint in dark blue and cream

crackle varnish

paint brushes

clock mechanism with plastic hands

14 cm (5½ in) square of mount board (backing board)

pencil

strong thread

double-sided tape

WORKING THE CROSS STITCH

Tack (baste) guidelines across the middle of the Aida in both directions. Work the backstitch using a single strand of cotton. Fill in the background with rows of cross stitch. Press on the reverse side when complete.

	Anchor
⊟	1223
	Backstitch
—	1223
☆	Middle point

1 To make up: drill a 10 mm (⅜ in) hole in the centre of the MDF. Mitre one end of the wood trim, measure 14 cm (5½ in) along the inside edge and mitre the other end. Saw another three pieces the same size. Spread glue on the underside and mitred edges of the wood trim and stick to the MDF. Tape the frame together and allow to dry, then sand the edges.

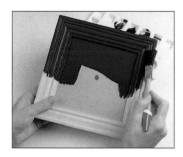

1 Paint the frame with dark blue paint. Let each layer dry before applying the next. Paint with a coat of crackle varnish, then with a coat of cream paint. The last coat can be dried with a hair dryer which will help the cracks to form. Trim the clock hands if necessary and paint in the same way.

2 Check that the mount board (backing board) fits inside the frame. Mark the position of the hole and cut one in the mount board. Stretch the embroidery over the board, mitring the corners neatly, and trim away any excess fabric. Cut into the fabric carefully and insert the front of the clock mechanism into the hole. Stick the mount board onto the frame and screw on the rest of the clock fitments.

YIANNI'S TAVERNA

*This peaceful seaside scene was inspired by a typical Greek taverna
and conjures up a summer holiday feeling.*

YOU WILL NEED

*45 x 50 cm (18 x 20 in) Antique
white 28 count evenweave linen*

tacking (basting) thread

needle

*stranded cotton DMC white,
350, 400, 435, 437, 598, 646,
648, 712, 747, 842, 988, 3024,
3348*

tapestry needle

*21 x 23 cm (8¼ x 9 in)
mount board (backing board)*

strong thread

picture frame

WORKING
THE CROSS STITCH

Tack (baste) guidelines
across the middle of the
linen in both directions and
work the cross stitch using
two strands of cotton. Press
carefully on the reverse side
when complete.

1 To make up: stretch the
embroidery over the
mount board (backing board)
and fit into a suitable picture
frame of your choice.

DMC	
⹀⹀	350
⸬⸬	400
⋗⋗	435
◇◇	437
⬘⬘	598
▽▽	646
∕∕	648
⟍⟍	712
⋃⋃	747
▲▲	988
⋉⋉	3024
✕✕	3348
◠◠	white
�	842

— Backstitch
646

☆ Middle point

KEY HOLDER

CONTEMPORARY

Keys have a habit of being in the wrong place at the wrong time.
This cleverly designed key holder will ensure that you do not lose them.

WORKING THE CROSS STITCH

As the quantities used are small, don't feel that you need to buy every thread listed for this project. Use stranded cotton from your own collection to match the colours shown. Stitch the different doors onto the Aidaplus, keeping the threads as neat as possible on the reverse side.

1 To make up: paint the blank key holder with two coats of paint. Allow to dry and then fit the supplied hooks and hanging ring.

2 Cut out the completed designs close to the stitching. Aidaplus doesn't fray, but take care not to cut any threads. Arrange on the base and glue in position

YOU WILL NEED

blank key holder

terracotta paint, Colourman 106

paintbrush

sheet of platinum Aidaplus, Zweigart

stranded cotton DMC 300, 301, 310, 350, 356, 422, 433, 451, 500, 503, 611, 613, 677, 729, 740, 798, 817, 926, 927, 928, 932, 977, 986,989, 3047, 3346, 3756, 3799, white

embroidery needle

scissors

all-purpose glue

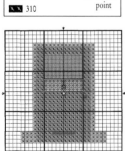

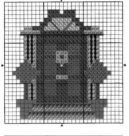

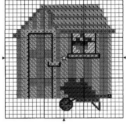

DMC		Backstitch
451	white	— 433
740	928	— 817
986	817	— 3799
989		☆ Middle point
310		

DMC		Backstitch
350	926	— 817
356	927	— 3799
433	928	
729	3047	☆ Middle point
817	3346	

DMC	Backstitch
611	— 611 ☆ Middle point
613	— 310
677	
928	French knots
932	611

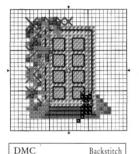

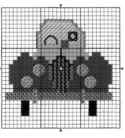

DMC	Backstitch
611	— 611 ☆ Middle point
613	— 310
677	French knots
928	
932	611

DMC		Backstitch
500	927	— 503
503	3756	— 3799
729	3799	
798		☆ Middle point
926		

ROMAN BLIND

This stunning blind is made all the more dramatic by the choice of bold striped fabric shaded from dark to light blue.

YOU WILL NEED

measuring tape

striped cotton fabric

25 cm (10 in) wide 10 count waste canvas

tacking (basting) thread

needle

stranded cotton DMC four skeins of 700, two skeins of 307 and one skein each of 105, 743, 995 (approximate quantities)

embroidery needle

pencil

ruler

binding tape

pins

sewing machine

sewing thread

scissors

fusible bonding web to fit size of blind

brass rings

2.5 x 5 cm (1 x 2 in) wood strip the width of the window

hand saw

tacks

hammer

screw eyes

fine non-stretch cord

2.5 cm (1 in) wooden batten the width of the window

cleat (for winding the cord round)

WORKING THE CROSS STITCH

Measure the height and width of your window and add 8 cm (3 in) to the width and 15 cm (6 in) to the length. You will need two pieces of fabric this size for the blind. Tack (baste) the waste canvas 15 cm (6 in) from the bottom of one piece of fabric. Mark the centre and work the cross stitch using three strands of cotton. Continue the design out towards each side, stopping after a complete tree. Fray the canvas and pull out the threads one at a time. Press on the reverse side when complete.

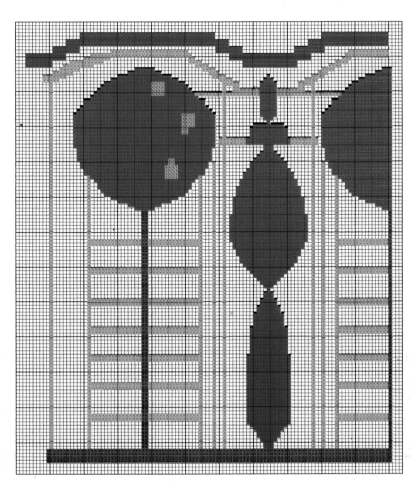

	DMC
	995
	700
	743
	105
	307

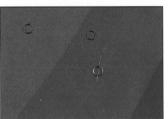

1 To make up: draw vertical lines down the right side of the lining fabric about 30 cm (12 in) apart with the outside lines about 8 cm (3 in) in from the edge. Pin and tack tape down all these lines and machine stitch down both sides. Iron fusible bonding web to the reverse side of the embroidered fabric. Remove the backing paper and lay the lining on top. Making sure the fabric is flat, press the layers together.

2 Turn in a 2.5 cm (1 in) hem down both sides of the blind and stitch. Turn up and stitch a 4 cm (1½ in) hem along the bottom edge. Making sure they are quite level, sew rings to the tapes every 15 cm (6 in) starting just above the hem.

3 Cut a headboard to fit the width of the window. Hammer in tacks to fix the top of the blind to the edge of the board. Fix screw eyes to the underside of the board so that they line up with the rings on the blind. The last ring on the right hand side should be large enough to take all the cords.

TO FINISH

Thread a length of cord through the large screw eye and down through the first line of rings. Knot it to the bottom ring. Thread cords through the other lines of rings in the same way, bring the cords together, and then tie a knot just below the large screw eye and plait the excess cord. Tie a knot at the end and trim. Slip the batten into the bottom hem and slip stitch both ends. Fit the heading board above the window and screw the cleat in at a comfortable height.

CHAMBRAY PILLOWCASE

Monograms give bed linen a touch of class. Choose your own initials to stitch in the corner of a classic Oxford pillowcase.

YOU WILL NEED

chambray Oxford pillowcase

small embroidery frame (flexihoop)

10 cm (4 in) square of 10 count waste canvas

stranded cotton Anchor 2

tacking (basting) thread

embroidery needle

white stranded cotton

Anchor	
■■	342

WORKING THE CROSS STITCH

Fit the embroidery hoop (frame) inside the pillow case and tack (baste) the canvas in the corner. Work the cross stitch design using three strands of cotton.

1 Once complete, fray and remove the canvas threads one at a time. Press on the reverse side. Stitch the same monogram on the corner of a matching sheet or duvet cover.

MINIATURE PICTURE

These tiny frames are very popular and this design would make
a delightful gift for a partner or friend.

WORKING THE CROSS STITCH

Fit the linen into the frame
(flexihoop) and work the cross
stitch border using a single strand
of cotton over two threads.
Complete the heart and work the
backstitch to finish the design
and press on the reverse side.

1 To make up: remove the back from the
frame and use the card insert to mount
the embroidery. Stick the wadding (batting) to
the card, trim the embroidery to an 8 cm (3 in)
square and stretch the fabric over the wadding,
sticking it down on the reverse side.

2 Fit the embroidery into the frame.
Add another layer of card (cardboard) if
required and fit the back.

YOU WILL NEED

*15 cm (6 in) square of
36 count linen*

*small embroidery frame
(flexihoop)*

*stranded cotton Anchor 133,
152, 226, 289*

tapestry needle

*ready-made frame with a 5 cm
(2 in) window*

*6 cm (2½ in) square of
wadding (batting)*

double-sided tape

scissors

	Anchor		Backstitch
5 5	289	—	226
7 7	152		
8 8	133	☆	Middle
↑ ↑	226		point

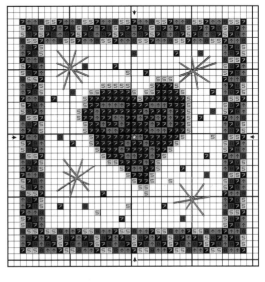

CAFETIERE COVER

Keep fresh coffee warm with this stylish cover, designed to fit a standard one-litre (two-pint) cafetière.

YOU WILL NEED

20 x 36 cm (8 x 14 in) white 14 count Aida

tacking (basting) thread

needle

interlocking bar frame

stranded cotton Anchor 148, 360, 370, 373, 398, 846

tapestry needle

scissors

30 cm (12 in) blue and white patterned fabric

15 x 28 cm (6 x 11 in) wadding (batting)

pins

sewing machine

sewing thread

bodkin

WORKING THE CROSS STITCH

Tack (baste) guidelines across the middle of the Aida in both directions and work the cross stitch using two strands of cotton. Once complete, work the backstitch and press the embroidery on the reverse side.

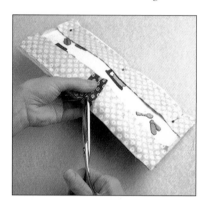

1 To make up: cut the embroidered panel and a piece of patterned fabric the same size as the wadding (batting). Tack the layers together with the wadding in between the fabrics. Cut three 6 x 38 cm (2½ x 15 in) strips of patterned fabric. With right sides facing, pin one piece along the bottom edge of the cover. Cut the other two strips in half. Cut a "v" in the centre of the top seam allowance. Fold over a 5 mm (¼ in) turning at one end of two of the short strips and butt the folds in the centre. Pin and tack along the top edge, and stitch using a 12 mm (½ in) seam allowance.

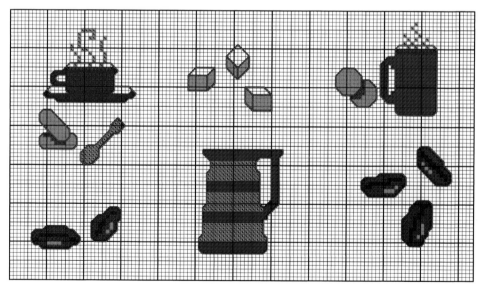

Anchor			Backstitch
846	360	398	— 360
373	370	148	

2 Turn under 12 mm (1/2 in) and fold the bindings to the reverse side. Pin and tack in position. Snip the top fold of the binding and tuck the end inside. Slip stitch along each side of the "v" and along the edges of the binding.

3 Cut two bias strips of patterned fabric about 30 cm (12 in) long and make them into rouleaux. Tack one to the middle of each side with the long end facing onto the cover. Pin and tack (baste) the remaining binding strips to the sides. Stitch to the edge of the top and bottom bindings. Trim the ends, turn in and fold the binding to the reverse side. Slip stitch the binding to complete the cafetière cover.

SHELF BORDER

*Stitch this smart teddy bear border, sewing a different coloured
bow tie on each bear, and make a matching cushion.*

YOU WILL NEED

*10 cm (4 in) wide Aida band
with red edges, Zweigart E7195*

measuring tape

scissors

pins

tacking (basting) thread

needle

*stranded cotton Anchor 369,
370, 403
for bow ties 4, 6; 38, 42; 108,
111; 217, 208; 293, 297*

tapestry needle

sewing thread

*double-sided tape or coloured
drawing pins*

WORKING THE CROSS STITCH

Measure the length of the shelf and
cut a piece of Aida band the same
length plus 5 cm (2 in) for turnings.
Each bear is about 8 cm (3 in) wide.
Decide on the spacing of the bears and
mark the centre line of each with a
pin. Tack (baste) guidelines across the
band at each pin and again along the
middle of the band to mark the centre
of each bear. Work the cross stitch
using two strands of cotton, changing
the colours in the bow ties on each
bear. Once complete, work the
backstitch using two strands of cotton
and press on the reverse side.

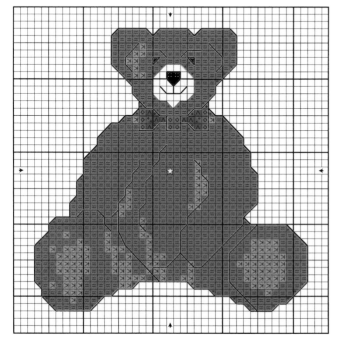

1 To make up: trim and turn under a
narrow hem at each end of the band.
You could either use coloured drawing
pins or double-sided tape to fix the border
in position on the shelf.

❖ ❖ ❖ ❖ ❖

NEEDLECRAFT TIP

To make a matching cushion panel,
divide a 40 cm (16 in) square of 7
count canvas in four. Allowing a 5 cm (2
in) margin round the outside edge,
cross stitch a bear in the middle of
each square using tapestry wool, and
fill in the background to match
the decor of the room.

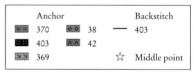

Anchor			Backstitch
══ 370	◇◇	38	—— 403
▓▓ 403	▲▲	42	
▷▷ 369			☆ Middle point

CHILD'S WAISTCOAT

*Denim can be given a much softer appearance with the addition
of some simple appliqué flowers and big bold cross stitches.*

WORKING THE CROSS STITCH

Using the vanishing marker pen, measure and mark dots every 1.5 cm (⅝ in) round the front and bottom edges of the waistcoat. Sew large pink cross stitches using all six strands of cotton, slipping the needle between the layer of denim to get to the next mark. Sew two tiny back stitches on the reverse side to secure the thread, and trim neatly.

YOU WILL NEED

child's denim waistcoat

vanishing marker pen

ruler

stranded cotton Anchor 254, 894, 939

embroidery needle

scraps of cotton fabric

15 cm (6 in) square of fusible bonding web

scissors

four small 4-hole buttons

1 To make up: iron fusible bonding web onto the reverse side of the fabric scraps and cut out 16 petals. Remove the paper backing and iron the petals in position on the pockets and on the back of the waistcoat. Sew the petals in place with cross stitches.

2 Sew a button in the middle of each flower with blue stranded cotton. Sew a small green cross stitch in the corners of the top pocket and a row along the top of the lower pockets. Thread blue stranded cotton underneath the cross stitches on the pockets to finish.

CHILD'S BAG

This bag will appeal to all ages and will become a firm favourite with children and young teenagers to hold their bits and pieces.

YOU WILL NEED

28 x 100 cm (11 x 39 in) blue gingham

scissors

stranded cotton Anchor 225, 311, 894, 1028

embroidery needle

5 x 25 cm (2 x 10 in) pink denim

fusible bonding web

18 x 46 cm (7 x 18 in) blue denim

pins

sewing machine

sewing thread

tacking (basting) thread

1.5 cm (⁵⁄8 in) button

WORKING THE CROSS STITCH

Cut a piece of gingham about 10 x 14 cm (4 x 5¹⁄2 in) and press under a small 1 cm (³⁄8 in) turning all round. Using three strands of cotton, sew the cross stitch border. Iron fusible bonding web onto the reverse side of a 5 cm (2 in) square of pink denim. Cut out three small hearts, remove the backing paper and iron onto the gingham. Sew in place with tiny stitches and stitch a blue cross in the middle of each heart to complete. Press on the reverse side.

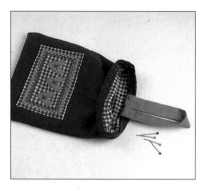

1 To make up: fold the blue denim in half crossways and open out. Pin the gingham patch on the top half and stitch. With the embroidery to the inside, fold the denim in half again and stitch both sides. Make a slightly narrower gingham lining in the same way and insert into the bag. Turn over a 2.5 cm (1 in) hem. With right sides facing, fold the pink denim strip in half lengthways and stitch the long edge. Trim and press the seam open, then turn through and press again with the seam at the centre back. Fold the strip to make a loop and pin under the hem at the centre back. Tack in position then stitch round the lower edge of the hem. Fold the loop back on itself and stitch.

2 Cut an 8 x 100 cm (3 x 39 in) strip of gingham and sew large cross stitches up the middle. Fold lengthways with the embroidery to the inside and stitch the long seam. Trim and press the seam open, then turn through and press again with the seam down the centre back. Turn under 12 mm (¹⁄2 in) at each end of the strap and pin over the side seams. Tack (baste) and stitch securely. Sew the button on the front of the bag and sew a large cross stitch to hold the loop flat.

KITCHEN HANGING

Kitchens are busy places and often neglected, but you could change things by making this delightful decoration to hang on the wall.

YOU WILL NEED

15 x 30 cm (6 x 12 in) cream 28 count evenweave linen

scissors

tacking (basting) thread

needle

interlocking bar frame

stranded cotton DMC 312, 316, 435, 743, 3802, 3815, 3823

tapestry needle

sewing machine

sewing thread

two 11 cm (4⅜ in) squares of wadding (batting)

5 cm (2 in) of 15 mm (⅝ in) ribbon or tape

pins

40 cm (16 in) plant support or 46 cm (18 in) of wire with the ends bent over

bay leaves and dried apple slices

WORKING THE CROSS STITCH

Cut the linen in half crossways. Tack (baste) guidelines across the middle of one piece in both directions and work the cross stitch using two strands of cotton over two threads. Once complete, work the backstitch using one strand of cotton and then press on the reverse side.

DMC		
═ ═ 3802	▼ ▼ 3815	
▓ 312	‖ ‖ 3823	
▷ ▷ 316	Backstitch	
◇ ◇ 435	— 3823	
✕ ✕ 743	☆ Middle point	

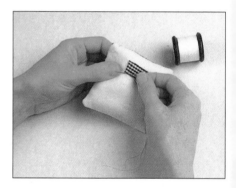

1 To make up: with the embroidery facing in, sew the two pieces of linen together. Stitch two threads away from the cross stitch and leave a 5 cm (2 in) gap at the bottom. Trim the seams and corners and turn through. Tuck the wadding inside and slip stitch the gap. Fold over the ends of the ribbon and pin to the back of the cushion, 2 cm (¾ in) down from the top. Oversew on both long sides.

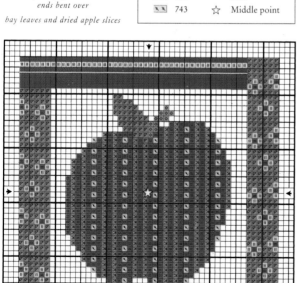

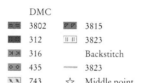

2 Thread the cushion onto the wire loop. Make small holes in the bay leaves and thread onto the wire with slices of dried apple in between. Some of the larger bay leaves are bent over and threaded through again to create a looser effect. Oversew the corners of the cushion to hold them secure, loop over the ends of the wire and hang in the kitchen.

POT HOLDER

This colourful and stylish tile design was inspired by the lemon trees and deep blue sea of the Mediterranean.

YOU WILL NEED

15 cm (6 in) square of white 14 count Aida

tacking (basting) thread

needle

interlocking bar frame

stranded cotton DMC 307, 322, 336

tapestry needle

scissors

pins

two 23 cm (9 in) squares of dark blue chintz (glazed cotton)

sewing machine

sewing thread

10 cm (4 in) navy cord

10 cm (4 in) cushion pad

WORKING THE CROSS STITCH

Tack (baste) guidelines across the middle of the Aida in both directions and work the cross stitch using two strands of cotton. Press on the reverse side once complete.

1 To make up: trim the Aida to a 13 cm (5 in) square, mitre the corners and turn under 12 mm (½ in) on all sides. Pin, tack and stitch in the centre of one piece of chintz (glazed cotton). Fold the cord in half and sew it, loop facing in, to one of the corners.

DMC		
☰☰	307	☆ Middle point
▓	322	
▓	336	

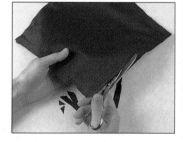

2 With right sides facing, sew the pieces of chintz together, with a gap on one side. Trim the seams and across the corners and turn through.

3 Insert the cushion pad and pin in the middle of the cover. Tack round the edges of the cushion pad and stitch. Slip stitch the gap closed to finish.

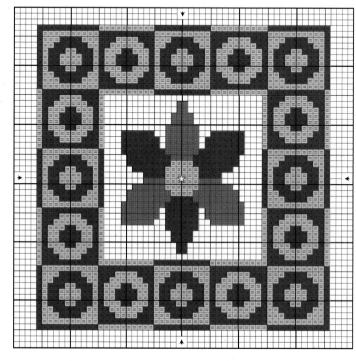

RUCKSACK

Rucksacks are extremely useful bags for all kinds of activities.
Sew the zebra panel to your own bag
or make this one following the easy instructions.

YOU WILL NEED

20 x 25 cm (8 x 10 in) white 18 count Aida

tacking (basting) thread

needle

interlocking bar frame

stranded cotton Anchor white, 22, 189, 297, 399, 403, 410

tapestry needle

paper

pencil

scissors

pins

From 1.50 m (1⅝ yd) of 115 cm (45 in) wide berry canvas, cut the following pieces: a 31 x 77 cm (12 x 30 in) back panel; a 56 x 77 cm (22 x 30 in) front panel; a 31 x 13 cm (12 x 5 in) base; two 28 x 19 cm (11 x 7 in) flap pieces; and two 8 x 69 cm (3 x 27 in) straps

sewing machine

sewing thread

four large "D" rings

10 large eyelets and tool

white cotton cord

button

14 x 18 cm (5½ x 7 in) fusible bonding web

WORKING THE CROSS STITCH

Tack (baste) guidelines across the middle of the Aida in both directions and work the cross stitch border using two strands of cotton. Next, work the zebra design and press on the reverse side once complete.

1 To make up the rucksack: pin the front and back panels together down both long sides and stitch together. Press the seams flat and fold in half with the seams to the inside. Tack the raw edges together, matching the seams. Top stitch round the folded edge and again 5 cm (2 in) away. Cut two 5 x 15 cm (2 x 6 in) pieces from the remaining canvas. Turn under 12 mm (½ in) on the long sides, fold in half and top stitch down both sides. Slide two "D" rings onto each strap, fold the straps in half and pin, with the rings facing onto the bag.

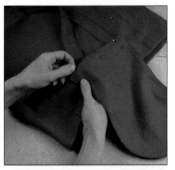

2 Pin and tack the base to the bottom of the bag. Snip the corners and stitch. Pin the flap pieces together and cut a half circle at one of the shorter sides to form a curved edge. Sew around the curved edge, trim the seam and snip the curves. Turn through. Roll the seam between your fingers then press and top stitch. For the straps, fold under a short end, then make as before. Pin and tack the raw edge between the seams and just below the second top stitching line. Pin the bag flap on top. Stitch across the flap, fold it over the raw edges and stitch a rectangle to secure.

3 Mark the position of the eyelets round the top of the rucksack and fit them following the manufacturer's directions. Thread a cord through the eyelets and tie 5 cm (2 in) from each end. Unravel the cord at the ends to make tassels. Make a buttonhole on the bag flap and sew a button in place.

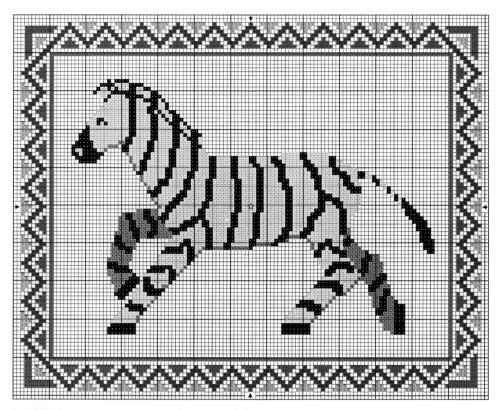

Anchor		
■ ■ 403	□ □	22
▨ ▨ 399	■ ■	189
− − white		
⑤ ⑤ 297	☆	Middle
⊠ ⊠ 410		point

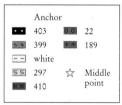

TO FINISH

Iron fusible bonding web onto the back of the cross stitch. Peel off the backing paper and pin the panel to the front of the bag. Press on the reverse side and back-stitch with 22 round the panel, one row out from the last stitching. Once the panel is complete, trim to about 1.5 cm (⅝ in) and fray the Aida.

BACKGROUND
MOUNT

CONTEMPORARY

*The exquisite embroidery makes a beautiful background for a small
Christmas wreath which can be renewed each year.*

YOU WILL NEED

*30 cm (12 in) square of gold
fleck 14 count Lurex Aida,
Zweigart E3287*

tacking (basting) thread

needle

embroidery hoop (frame)

*fine gold braid Kreinik 221,
2122*

stranded cotton Anchor 923

blending filament Kreinik 008

tapestry needle

*2 m (2⅓ yd) of 3 mm (⅛ in)
green ribbon*

pins

*Virginia creeper or clematis
stems*

wax gilt

*small poppy heads, star anise
and cupressus cones*

all-purpose glue or glue gun

mount board (backing board)

strong thread

picture frame

WORKING
THE CROSS STITCH

Tack (baste) guidelines
across the middle of the
Aida in both directions.
Work the cross stitch using
the fine braid, as it comes,
and two strands of cotton
with the blending filament.
Lay the ribbon diagonally
across the embroidered
panel. Pin and tack it
securely in position at both
ends, then sew an upright
cross stitch with fine braid
221 where the ribbons
overlap. Block the design
when it is completed.

1 To make up: cut several fairly long lengths of
creeper and coil them into a 15 cm (6 in) circle.
Take another length of creeper and wrap this round
and round the wreath to hold the coils together
securely. Tuck the ends inside to complete the wreath.

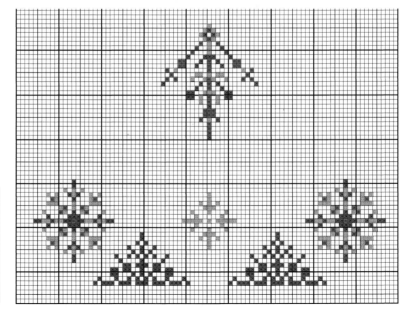

Balger Fine Braid

221

2122

Balger Blending
Filament 008
+ Anchor 923

Stretch the embroidery over the mount board (backing board). Lay the wreath in position. Sew strong thread through the board in several places, taking it back through close to the original holes, and tie the ends securely. Fit into a frame of your choice.

2 Using your finger, wipe some wax gilt over the surface of the wreath. Once the wax gilt is dry it can be buffed gently with a soft cloth.

3 Arrange the dried plant material round the wreath until you are satisfied with the position, then glue. You can add more tendrils from the creeper, too. When the glue has dried, wipe more wax gilt over the plant material.

EGG CABINET

Eggs keep much better at room temperature than in the fridge.
This little cabinet with a broody hen on the front is ideal.

YOU WILL NEED

25 cm (10 in) square of pinky beige 28 count Jobelan

tacking (basting) thread

needle

embroidery hoop (frame)

wildflower cotton one skein each of terracotta/dark blue and spice

stranded cotton DMC white, 816, 841, 842, 3031

tapestry needle

egg cabinet with a 15 cm (6 in) door opening

paint, Colourman 104, 109, 114 (optional)

paintbrush

rubber gloves

medium steel wool

15 cm (6 in) square of mount board (backing board)

strong thread

15 cm (6 in) square of hardboard

panel pins

hammer

WORKING THE CROSS STITCH

Wildflower cotton is a variegated colour thread, not unlike flower thread or Nordin in weight and appearance. Open out the terracotta yarn and cut out the darkest blue sections. Work the main body of the hen in the variegated wildflower cotton and the shadows and head details in the blue.

Tack (baste) guidelines across the middle of the linen in both directions and work the cross stitch using one strand of wildflower cotton. Using two strands of stranded cotton, work the rest of the cross stitch. Once complete, work the backstitch and then press on the reverse side.

	DMC
--	white
10	3031
22	841+842
33	841
HH	816
	Wildflower
■■	Terracotta/dark blue
✕✕	Spice
⊐⊐	Terracotta/ dark blue (removed)
	Backstitch ~ DMC
—	841
☆	Middle point

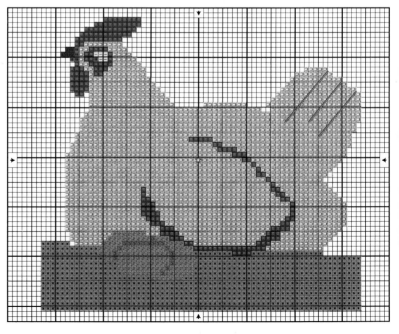

Stretch the embroidery
over the mount board
(backing board) and fit
inside the door frame.
Fit a square of
hardboard at the back
and fix in place with
panel pins.

1 To make up: paint the egg cabinet
with blue paint and allow it to dry
completely. Paint on top with the cream
paint. You may need to add a touch of
terracotta paint to tone the final look in
with the linen.

2 Wearing rubber gloves to protect
your hands, rub down the cabinet to
reveal some of the blue paint and give the
cabinet a "distressed" look. Brush out all
the loose dust and wipe down with a
barely damp cloth.

GIFT BAG

This luxurious bag with its hand-stitched monogram makes a very personal and beautiful wrapping for a special gift.

YOU WILL NEED

two 15 x 25 cm (6 x 10 in) pieces of metallic organza

sewing machine

sewing thread

two 15 x 25 cm (6 x 10 in) pieces of burgundy silk dupion (mid-weight silk)

scissors

pins

tacking (basting) thread

needle

5 cm (2 in) square of 14 count waste canvas

Anchor Marlitt 1034

stranded cotton Anchor 150

embroidery needle

46 cm (18 in) navy cord

bodkin

two navy tassels

1 To make up: fold over a 5 cm (2 in) hem on the short sides of the organza pieces and stitch down 4 cm (1½ in) on both sides. Repeat with the silk but turn up 1 cm (¼ in) of the hem before stitching. Trim across the corners, snip into the bottom of the stitching and turn through. With both hems facing the reverse side, layer the silk and organza together. Stitch across the hem twice, 1 cm (⅜ in) apart, to form a casing. Pin and tack (baste) the waste canvas in the bottom right corner, 6 cm (2⅜ in) from the raw edges.

2 Work the cross stitch using two strands of Marlitt and the backstitch using two strands of cotton. Once the embroidery is complete, remove the canvas threads one at a time. Press on the reverse side. Pin both sections together with right sides facing, and stitch round the three sides. Zigzag close to the stitching to neaten and trim the seam.

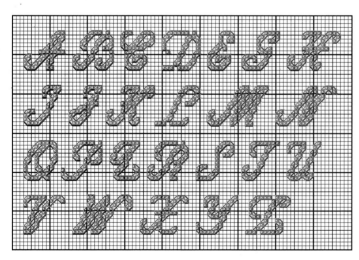

Anchor Marlitt	Backstitch ~ Anchor
3 3 1034	—— 150

3 Turn the bag through and thread the cord through the casing with a bodkin. Slip one tassel over both cords to use as a fastening. Thread the other tassel onto one end of the cord. Overlap the ends of the cord and sew them together. Pull the cord gently until the join is inside the casing.

CHRISTMAS DECORATIONS

These unusual decorations are easy to make and can be strung along a mantelpiece or hung on the tree.

YOU WILL NEED

5 x 15 cm (2 x 6 in) 22 count single canvas

gold spray paint

Anchor Marlitt 844, 1036

fine gold braid Kreinik 221

tapestry needle

white and burgundy handmade paper

scissors

pins

ruler

paper cord

all-purpose glue

single hole punch

WORKING THE CROSS STITCH

Cut the canvas in three, spray both sides with gold paint and allow to dry. Work a different motif in the middle of each, using two strands of cotton and the fine braid as it comes.

Anchor Marlitt		Kreinik Fine Gold Braid
3 3	1036	
4 4	844	○ ○ 221
—	844	— 221

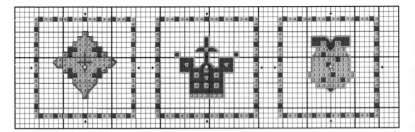

1 To make up: cut three 7 cm (2¾ in) squares of burgundy paper and pin the embroidered canvas in the centre. Work the cross stitch border through both layers, keeping the stitches two threads in from the edge.

2 Hold the ruler down flat on the white paper and use it to tear off three 10 cm (4 in) squares. Spray the paper cord and the white paper squares lightly with gold paint. Glue the burgundy paper squares onto the white paper and punch two holes at the top. Thread the cord through the holes to finish the decorations.

ACKNOWLEDGEMENTS & SUPPLIERS

The author and publishers would like to thank the following contributors for their projects:

Jenny Blair
p138, 248

Lynda Burgess
p228, 238

Alison Burton
p126, 132

Sally Burton
p196, 206, 239, 240

Christine Coggan
p98

Vanessa Donnelly
p46

Allison Duncan
p38, 232

Lucinda Ganderton
p65, 112, 158, 161, 166, 170, 172

Joyce Graham
p117

Lesley Grant
p42, 128, 174, 194, 212, 214, 231

Mary Handley
p234, 250

Kate Hanson-Smith
p96, 120

Alison Harper
p152, 177, 189, 190

Lucie Heaton
p157, 242

Rachel Hyde
p67, 68, 183

Steven Jenkins
p40, 41, 44, 53, 57, 60, 61, 64, 77, 82, 86, 98, 102, 130, 142, 143, 202, 211, 236

Caroline Kelly
p92, 134, 160, 164, 197

Maureen Kennaugh
p70, 84

Claire Metson
p72, 111, 136

Linda Mitchell
p220

Jennie Parry
p180

Penelope Randall
p48, 215

Jane Rimmer
p54, 127, 176

Denise Roberts
p86, 184

Brenda Sandford-Monk
p80

Carolyn Sibbald
p49, 57, 73, 141, 192, 198

Barbara Smith
p106

Zoe Smith
p122, 124

Julia Tidmarsh
p74, 84, 191, 222, 230, 244

Carol Tompkins
p178

Hilary Walton
p50, 58

Christine Watkin
p66, 88

Angela Wheeler
p78, 167

Sue Whiting
p94, 100, 104, 114, 115, 119, 131

Barley Wood
p246

Thanks also to Bridgette Ainsworth, Mavis Blake, Linda Fraser and Barry Sims for their help in making some of the projects.

All other projects were designed and made by the author.

Useful addresses and suppliers

UNITED KINGDOM

Coats Craft UK
PO Box 22
The Lingfield Estate
McMullen Road
Darlington
DL1 1YQ
Consumer Services Helpline
01325 365457
Embroidery threads, Kreinik metallic threads and fabrics

DMC Creative World Ltd
Pullman Road
Wigston
Leicestershire
LE18 2DY
0116 2811040
Embroidery thread, Zweigart fabrics and bands

Artisan Needlecrafts
Battlers Green Farm
Common Lane
Radlett
Hertfordshire
WD7 8PH
01923 853327
Easy grid and fabri

The Inglestone Collection
Yells Yard
Cirencester Road
Fairford
Gloucestershire
GL7 4BS
01285 712778
Linen bands and stitching paper

Janik Enterprises Ltd
Brickfield Lane
Denbigh Road
Ruthin
Clwyd
LL15 2TN
01824 702096
Wood blanks, round wood box

Decorative Arts Company
5a Royal Crescent
London
W11 4SL
0171 3714303
Clock base, key holder, papier mâché boxes

AB Woodworking
Unit J
Pentre Wern
Gobowen
Oswestry
Shropshire
SY10 7JZ
01691 670425
Shaker box

Knot Just Wood
Wooten Wawen
Solihull
01789 450889
Egg cabinet

Framecraft
372/376 Summer Lane
Hockley
Birmingham
B19 3QA
0121 2120551
Frosted bowl, tray and pot stand

Pinebrush Products
Coton Clanford
Stafford
ST18 9PB
01785 282799
Reproduction paints

C'est Ça
4c St Mary's Works
Duke Street
Norwich
NR3 1QA
Kitchen apron

Offray Ribbon
Customer Services
0171 631 3548
Ribbons

Linda Edwards
Clare Maddicot Publications
Cambridge
BB1 2DW
01223 353 250
Cards and gift wrap

AUSTRALIA

Coats Patons Crafts Pty Ltd
89/91 Peters Avenue
Mulgrave Vic 3170
Customer Services
1800 801 195

DMC Needlecraft Pty Ltd
51/55 Carrington Road
Marrickville NSW 2204
(02) 559 3088
Needlecraft Mail Box
154 Mann Street
Gosford NSW 2250
Mail Order and Retail
1800 02 4942

Simply Stitches
153 Victoria Avenue
Chatswood NSW 2067
(02) 412 4342

Bargello
819 Glenferrie Road
Hawthorn Vic 3122
Mail order and retail
(03) 9818 4853

Lazy Daisy
(Needlework specialists)
142 Burgundy Street
Heidelberg Vic 3084
Retail plus mail order
(03) 9457 2322

Craft Ideas
Shop 2065
Westfield Shopping Town
Indoorpilly Qld 4068
(07) 3378 4288

UNITED STATES AND CANADA

Aardvark Adventures
PO Box 2449
Livermore
CA 94551
(800) 388 2687
Cross stitch and embroidery fabrics, threads and trims

Heartland Crafts Discounters
Rte 6E
PO Box 65
Genesco
IL61254
Threads, yarns, tools

Herrschers
Hoover Road
Stevens Point
WI 54481
(800) 441 0838
General needlecraft tools and materials

Nancy's Notions
PO Box 683
Dept 32
Beaver Dam
WI 53916
(414) 887 0391
Sewing, quilting, beadwork, appliqué, embroidery

Yarnworks
519 Main Street
Grand Junction
CO 81501
(303) 243 5365
Knitting, crochet, cross stitch, dyeing

Bettekaril's Needlecrafts
PO Box 5008
Brandon
MS 39047
(601) 992 3266
Cross stitch, crochet, knitting

INDEX

NOTES

NOTES

NOTES

NOTES

NOTES

NOTES

NOTES

NOTES